KU-737-428

Papers on Residential Work

Consultation in Child Care

Collected Papers by Barbara Dockar-Drysdale

With a Foreword by Robert Tod
Central Council for Education and
Training in Social Work

SOCIAL STUDIES
LIBRARY.
45, WELLINGTON SQUARE,
OXFORD.

SOCIAL STUDIES
WITHDRAWN
SOCIAL STUDIES CENTRE, GEORGE S
OXFORD. OX1 2RL

Longman

36217

Longman Group Limited
London

*Associated companies, branches and representatives
throughout the world*

© Longman Group Limited 1973

All rights reserved. No part of this publication may be reproduced,
stored in a retrieval system, or transmitted in any form or by any
means, electronic, mechanical, photocopying, recording, or otherwise,
without the prior permission of the Copyright owner.

First published 1973

ISBN 0 582 42848 3

Printed in Singapore by New Art Printing Co., (Pte.) Ltd.

To our children,
Sarah, William, Charles and Caroline

Contents

Foreword

If you are working closely with unhappy and angry children, or if you have responsibility for supporting and helping staff who are professionally involved with children, I believe that these papers will speak to your condition. Such work makes pressing demands on our personal resources, our caring and empathy, our insight and self-awareness. We need to draw upon our memories of childhood stress and apply what is valid from this to our own work with children. We need too the capacity to acknowledge the mutual dependence of members of staff on each other as well as the interdependence of staff and children. From time to time also it is important that we should make public what has hitherto been private and particular, and examine and test our practice and give our ideas to others in order to see if they are real and reliable.

This is the exercise on which Mrs Dockar-Drysdale has been engaged in the last few years, and as we read this second collection of papers, originally given as spoken addresses, she communicates to us the essential unity of her feeling and thinking. The papers are based on her experience of therapeutic work with children or consultancy with staff, which has been informed and deepened by her own study, reflection and analysis, clarified by theory and here expressed in a statement. In reading her chapters, we are drawn into accompanying her in the process of experience, realization and conceptualization.

I found that the papers said most to me when I read them in a reflective way, pausing from time to time to compare her insights with my own experience or to match, if I could, her clinical illustrations with situations I had encountered. I am sure that those readers who are involved with disturbed children in a residential setting will repeatedly find their own experience refocused or given significance by the discoveries made or clarification given by Mrs Dockar-Drysdale.

The present book carries further the experience and theoretical concepts presented and discussed in the author's first volume of papers, *Therapy in child care*. Readers will find that knowledge of the papers in the first book provides a necessary background to understanding these further papers. The present book is much more than a restatement of previous theories. In reading it I was constantly impressed by the way in which Mrs Dockar-Drysdale's thinking, founded on the work of others, has moved on and developed, so that here original concepts are presented in a new context for the first time.

At the risk of anticipating the contents of the book, I should like to mention those new concepts or insights which caught my imagination or confirmed my own experience: the classification of stress into simple stress uncomplicated by guilt which is bearable and complex stress which can be sometimes intolerable (ch. 1); the disabling effect upon staff of the force of unconscious envy (chs. 1 and 10); the need of visiting parents for a 'safe place' within the residential establishment, (ch. 2); the acceptance of there being no clear lines of demarcation between the therapist and the patient, the staff and the child, all needing supportive relationships to enable them to develop as human beings (ch. 5); the study and analysis of the needs of children rather than of their symptomatic behaviour provided in the two chapters on Need Assessment (chs. 8 and 9); and the description of the delusional equilibrium which is found in some establishments, where the overt task is frustrated by the existence of an anti-task that is outwardly denied (ch. 10).

Other readers will find other aspects that are valuable to them, perhaps the clinical case studies that are always vivid and apropos of the introduction to the theories of other writers, D.W. Winnicott, Klein or Sechehaye.

Mrs Dockar-Drysdale believes that in therapeutic work with children, unexamined intuitions are not enough; our work with disturbed children must be conscious, disciplined and professional.

In publishing her papers, she is sharing with us her conscious and disciplined presentation and examination of her professional experience and working concepts. I believe that many practitioners in residential work will find in this book the stimulus and encouragement that they need to develop their own thinking and practice.

Robert Tod

January 1973

Introduction

This second collection of papers records my further experiences and thoughts concerning the therapy needed by emotionally deprived children in residential places. These later papers will certainly be easier to read if the first collection *Therapy in Child Care* is already familiar, but chapter 5, 'Meeting children's emotional needs' should cover most of the essential ground for readers who are not used to the concepts involved.

Most of my earlier work was carried out within the Mulberry Bush School (a school for maladjusted children which my husband and I founded many years ago): it has only been during the last four years that I have become aware of just how great is the number of unintegrated children in residential care. I have been working now for some time as a consultant to the Cotswold Community for delinquent adolescent boys, and have also been involved during the same period with a wide field of work in child care. I have come to prefer running workshops to giving lectures, so that many of the papers in this book have been a basis for a day's work with my audience. I have also discovered that it is pleasant to be interrupted – that is to say, I often ask my audience these days to stop me at any point which they would care to discuss with me.

The death of Dr D.W. Winnicott has been for me, as for so many others, an irreparable loss. I hope I have incorporated enough of what he taught me to continue to make use of his work.

I am most grateful to the many people with whom I can talk over experiences and realizations. I would especially like to thank Richard Balbernie and John Armstrong for all the help they have given me. My secretary Kate Britton has once again with unfailing skill and care arranged and edited these papers. Without all this help the book would not have been completed. None of us can work alone – perhaps this is the theme of this second collection of papers.

B. Dockar-Drysdale

January 1973

I

Problems arising in the communication of stress

I read this paper at a refresher course run by the Association of Workers for Maladjusted Children, in 1968. I had been for some time rather out of touch with the Association so that it was pleasant and stimulating to be talking with this particular audience once more. The discussion which followed the paper revealed the evolvement which has taken place during the last ten years in the treatment of disturbed children. I found myself thinking of our early days, and of how, although there was a long journey ahead, at least we had made a start on the right road.

The newborn baby expresses stress as soon as any inner or outer disturbance upsets its psychic equilibrium: this is as true of excitement as it is of pain. There is no need for communication to be established between mother and baby, because for the mother the baby's cry comes from within herself; she hears and responds to its need as she would to her own. If this primary maternal preoccupation is lacking from the start, the baby is doomed to emotional disorder, unless a mother substitute can take over who is capable of this preoccupation and can establish a primary unity.

A mother responds without thinking to delicate variations in tone and quality to her child's cry; what action she takes will depend on what she feels about the particular cry. People working with disturbed children in a residential place need to be able to feel a child's stress at this primitive level. I have heard people working in the Mulberry Bush say, 'There's Jenny crying again, but she's alright', or 'Quickly, I must get to Jenny – there's something wrong'. To an outsider there is little variation in the quality of Jenny's cry, but for people who are closely in touch with this borderline psychotic child (who often cries) there are nuances in the quality of her crying which they can feel because of their sensitive preoccupation with Jenny. This is something more primitive than empathy.

As babies develop, integrate into individuals in their own right, and begin to communicate verbally, the picture changes to some extent. A toddler who is wailing can explain through his tears that his teddy has disappeared, or that he has a pain in his tummy; his mother can help him to search for teddy, or to ease his pain or help him to endure it. Sometimes, however, the basic stress is not being directly communicated: the momentary loss of teddy may have triggered off a much deeper fear of losing his mother; the 'tummy ache' may be in itself much less painful for him than an underlying dread of dangerous 'bad' feelings or intolerable excitement inside him. His mother will intuitively respond to this deeper level also.

Severe stress remains, as at the beginning of life *unthinkable*. Panic is an extreme example of unthinkable stress: someone in a panic cannot communicate what he is feeling; it is only after he has recovered from the panic that he can gradually and with help begin to describe this awful phenomenon. This is true of adults as well as children. One could say that stress remains or becomes tolerable if and when it is communicable. Many people – grown-ups and children alike – can communicate stress in retrospect; few can do so while actually in a *state of stress*. They react, of course – much deviant behaviour is in an indirect way a statement of unendurable stress; but they may not have any insight into what has caused such breakdown in ego functioning. Everybody has his or her level of stress tolerance, depending on the degree to which his ego experience has enabled him to bend rather than break. Stress up to this level can have much positive value: many goals are reached under great but not intolerable stress.

The severely emotionally deprived children I shall be considering in this paper have a very low level of such tolerance. The skilled and deeply concerned grown ups who care for them can tolerate considerable stress before reaching breakdown.

The ability to communicate stress even in retrospect can help to raise the level of stress tolerance both for the consumers and the providers of primary experience. I use this term 'primary experience' to refer to experience belonging to the first year of life, without which integration as an individual is impossible. Primary experience may be given to the baby by the mother-figure, or may be offered at a later date by the therapist.

A group of people working with emotionally deprived children in a residential setting are extremely vulnerable. They are working in an involved and undefended way; only thus can they provide the primary experience needed. In this paper I shall only be considering grown ups and children *inside* the residential place. The problem of communication to outsiders is too big to consider here.

I do not consider that there can be a satisfactory emotional economy in a staff group in which there is no direct intercommunication of stress. Because realization and statement can make stress *thinkable*, i.e. containable (since through realization the underlying cause of the stress may become conscious), the insight gained may be available on later occasions.

A group of people working together in a residential place come to know the best and the worst in each other: they often meet (at meal times, for example) when one or more of the group may be in a state of great tension; the degree to which such a state can be communicated to others will depend on the emotional climate in the group.

Sometimes stress may be displaced, often from people to things: so that, for example, instead of bursting into tears over some awful experience with a child in a rage, the worker under stress may complain with tremendous force about the weather, or the food, or anything else.

Sometimes the whole group can sit eating in gloomy silence; in fact they are slowly recovering from stress. A newcomer, arriving for lunch on her second day's work at the Bush, commented, 'It was as though a dark cloud hung over the table – I didn't know what to do!' An alternative to this behaviour is for the group to make a flight to reality, chatting briskly at a surface level, while stress continues to churn around beneath. Sometimes, when the group is not too stress-loaded, one or more members can communicate their desperate state of what is often emotional impoverishment following too much tension. On these occasions other people in the group may be able to empathize with the sufferer. Reassurance is useless, of course, and only makes matters worse.

Here I am talking about the aftermath of stress. Often this is the only bit of the iceberg which is visible: we can but guess as to the real cause. By the time the stress is communicated, censorship may be seen in action. The worker communicates as much as he can bear to tell others without too much damage to his morale, prestige, or narcissism.

Winnicott, writing about the management of regression, points out that the strain involved is simple. I feel that we can make a useful distinction between *simple* and *complex* stress. Simple stress could be thought of as stress uncomplicated by guilt or other factors. For example, the stress experienced in sitting up all night with a child in a regression can be felt and communicated without guilt. If the child asks 'Are you tired?' the worker can reply 'Yes, I'm tired but I'm all right.' The circumstances of a regression are similar emotionally to those of early babyhood. The child is totally dependent on the therapist: the therapist is deeply involved with the child; and feeling something which is comparable to primary maternal preoccupation. Perhaps one of the most important characteristic features of such preoccupation is the lack of guilt. The ordinary devoted mother does not feel guilty in devoting herself to completely give to the needs of her baby; other people must take over her usual responsibilities for the time being: her stress is what I am describing as 'simple'. The worker involved in a regression has much the same experience, relying on colleagues to take over functions to enable him to sustain the role necessary for the child's regression.

If, however, a worker has been used (for example) as a reliable bad object through a long and exhausting evening by a very disturbed and testing child, then the worker may reach a stress level of angry resentment. He knows that if he is 'bad', another worker is probably 'good'. He is aware that this is a typical phenomenon at a certain stage of recovery; that he is doing valuable work by being reliably 'bad': yet because of the irritation and resentment at being used in this sort of way (for too long, perhaps) his state of stress is complicated by guilt. He is not sufficiently involved with the child for primary preoccupation to deal with the guilt (by projecting super-ego elements), so that he is not facing the simple stress I have described in connection with regression, but complex stress because of guilt experienced in respect of anger and resentment felt towards the child. These

4

are feelings which the worker would wish to disown; and which he may deny, repress or displace so that the resentment may turn up in some other area of experience. Simple stress is therefore fairly easy to communicate; but complex stress is another matter, because of the element of guilt or other factors which may not be conscious.

Many people coming into this field suppose that a good worker does not become cross, or frustrated, or tired. They consider that a professional view is an objective one; that a professional worker remains calm and detached; that the measure of skill and experience can be judged by the degree of such detachment. Unless they happen to have had a personal analysis they may suppose that analysis ensures this emotional equilibrium; that an analysed person does not experience stress. This confused attitude often leads the inexperienced worker to adopt a facade – a false-self defence. Such a worker often does his best to disguise stress, to present a calm, untroubled front in all circumstances; to communicate happenings, however devastating, in a cool and apparently objective manner; and above all, to avoid describing his own feelings in regard to such experiences. When in a discussion group, a student using this defence is likely to be shocked and disconcerted by other more mature workers' communication of anger, fear, or distress. He will speak of such reporting in a critical way, often suggesting that to talk in this way is evidence of emotional disturbance.

We are evolving[1] a type of reporting at the Mulberry Bush which attempts to avoid pseudo-objectivity, and to help us to accept the fact that happenings do not take place in isolation; that we are also involved, and that we can never observe without observing a situation observed (if we watch a mother bathing her baby, we are watching this happening *when observed*; even our presence alters the happening in many ways). The type of reporting to which I have referred implies an acceptance of the contribution which we may make to a situation, even though we may not say or do anything.

Parents are often unable to understand how much they contribute to their children's emotional state by stress which is not

[1] Since this paper was written, this technique has been established.

5

directly communicated to the child by words or actions. For example, a baby can catch his mother's depression: the symptoms which he may then develop may never be traced to their source. Very often, if we are able to tolerate insight, if we can dare to know that we are functioning under stress, we can then communicate our feelings to children directly, instead of (for example) projecting such feelings on to them; when we are angry with taking responsibility for our own feelings.

I have often mentioned an episode which made a deep impression on me during the first years of 'the Bush'. I was sitting on the steps leading down into a dormitory full of restless, hot children at about ten o'clock on a summer's night. I was waiting for the children to go to sleep, and becoming more and more frustrated, irritable and desperate as the time dragged on towards darkness. I tried to read – I had brought one of Freud's papers to occupy myself – but the children kept on murmuring and chattering to me and each other. They explained that they kept on talking because if they were to stop, I would go downstairs.

I grew more irritated, trying without success to read my book, and finally spoke very sternly to one of the talkers. 'Be quiet!' I said. 'It's late – very late, and there is to be no more of this.' I tried to sound calm and collected; the children knew better. Presently after a brief silence, one of them asked 'What *is* the matter with you?' I replied that I was hot and tired and cross. Whereupon the questioner said, 'Well, why don't you go downstairs and read your book, and let us go to sleep.' I accepted the offer and the children went to sleep at once: they had been acting out my hidden anger and frustration for me. Disturbed children are highly intuitive: they react in any adverse way to pseudo-objective responses from adults, often picking up the underlying stress.

Inexperienced workers such as I have described run into grave difficulties of this kind, often because they think that to be permissive is always to be therapeutic. The outcome of pseudo-objectivity and false professional calm and detachment tends to be major or minor breakdown, sometimes into panic states or psychosomatic symptoms. It can be important to realize that anger, hate or anxiety, when acknowledged and communicated, are far less likely to be acted out either by ourselves or through the children; and that a child can be deeply reassured by the discovery that, on occasions, we may even hate him, but that this does not mean that we *withdraw concern* from him – we continue to try to meet his needs.

Children can sometimes communicate stress in a vivid way. Peter, a six-year-old at the Bush some years ago, described to me how he felt when furious with somebody whom he was afraid to attack. He said, 'It feels dreadful – like as if I'm a hedgehog with the prickles sticking *in* instead of out.'

Tom, a thirteen-year-old delinquent, communicated an experience of extreme stress, in retrospect twenty-four hours later. He explained: 'I felt queer inside, especially in my stomach. It made me think of what you said about excitement and pinching – the feeling was excitement. I've often had it, but didn't think of it like that. I thought I'd buy some sweets: I went to the tuck shop, but it was shut. The feeling got worse: I sat on the edge of my bed, I didn't know where to put myself. I had a shower, but it didn't do any good. Then I thought of roller skates, but there wasn't anyone to lend me a pair. I went on getting worse, then someone came back and let me use his skates. I went very fast, specially round corners. I got better: the feeling went'.

Stress frequently produces physical symptoms; the nature of which can help us to understand the deeper cause. I asked Tom whether he thought there could be a connection between the awful feeling and something that could have happened in babyhood. I described a baby getting desperately excited waiting for his mother to feed him, and his mother not coming at the right time, and the baby getting more and more excited; by the time she did come Tom interrupted at this point, exclaiming, 'He wouldn't want the *feed*!' I said I thought that the baby would be hungry, but that the excitement and splendid greed would have got split off from the food, where it belonged; and that if this often happened, such a baby would lose excitement connected with food, and feel it elsewhere not connected with anything, as free-floating stress. I suggested that his delinquency was a way of dealing with this isolated excitement, and that perhaps it might be possible to link excitement to food in some way. He told me that he was never interested in his food. We then worked out a plan together which would help him.

7

I have quoted this episode in some detail because Tom's undefended communication of stress made it possible to give him much needed therapeutic help. If Tom has not been able to allow me to know about what was going on inside him, I could only have guessed at the nature of the problem. The fact that he could give me an accurate description of stress in action within him showed me the nature of this stress and enabled us both to understand the task ahead; the need to link the excitement with food, where it originally belonged, instead of delinquent activity.

Jenny made a deeply felt protest against complex stress. She needed at one time to cry, and for her crying to be accepted as a direct communication of anguish. However, some workers found her grief intolerable, giving her reassurance and trying to cheer her up, instead of accepting this communication of sorrow and pain. Jenny tried to adapt to these demands, but was too distressed to succeed. She said to me: 'I do wish people wouldn't *cheer me down.*' This was a vivid description of an attempt to complicate stress by mechanisms of flight or denial.

There are other contexts in which grown-ups find acknowledgement of stress intolerable. For example, the kind of collusion which goes on when a grown-up has to inflict pain on a child, saying 'There's a brave boy!' instead of 'I'm sorry I had to hurt you so badly': the boy has to be stoical because of the grown-up's needs.

Johnny cut his hand and had to have stitches in the Casualty Department of a large hospital. There was a lot of pain involved which he bore with a terrible stoicism. This was troubling to Vanno, a member of the Bush team, who was with him. The doctor and the nurse congratulated Johnny on his courage—he was now like a piece of granite—whereupon Vanno said quietly, 'Johnny, you do know don't you, that it's all right for you to cry?' Johnny broke out into helpless sobbing, buried his head in Vanno and collapsed. It is difficult for many people to understand that such breakdown can be necessary and therapeutic; that without this communication of stress there will be trouble later.

Much more common is the communication of stress in a more disguised form, often by means of symbolization. Jeffrey, who was epileptic as well as being severely emotionally deprived, came

8

to me in a very anxious state just after his arrival in the school. After several tentative questions he asked me whether I knew the rhyme of Humpty Dumpty. I replied that if Humpty Dumpty fell off the wall in the Bush we would try to pick up and hold all the bits. His relief confirmed my impression that he was speaking about his fits, which for him represented disintegration. Here is a symbolic communication of stress; which is, I think, usually best met by symbolic response.

In all these cases children have tried, fairly successfully, to communicate complex stress.

1. Peter, the hedgehog child felt prickles turned against himself, because he had to cope with aggression which he dared not express.
2. Tom's excitement had not been recognized by him as excitement, because this feeling was split off as a defence against intolerable waiting.
3. Jenny was able to continue her direct communication of simple stress because she was unable to make use of mechanisms of flight and denial.
4. In Johnny's case, grown-ups *needed* the child in pain to be stoical; as soon as he was given permission to feel hurt, he reacted in an emotionally appropriate way.
5. Jeffrey could communicate his stress in symbolic terms sufficiently clearly to be understood.

Children often express stress through non-verbal communication. They may scream, cry, cling, or become destructive: they may run away, climb a tree, or throw themselves on the ground. The response most likely to succeed is 'holding'; a technique used indiscriminately at Warrendale[1], but which can nevertheless prove valuable if used with discretion and in an appropriate context.

All of us are acutely aware of the dangers of institutionalization. Many of the children who come into our schools have been institutionalized following severe emotional deprivation during the first year of life. I think we can usefully consider the effect of institutional treatment on communication. One of the characteristics of severely deprived children is the inability to commu-

---

[1] Film: 'Warrendale', Allan King, 1967

9

nicate stress, which must nevertheless break through in the form of grossly deviant behaviour. An institution with a rigid organization forbids stress to be communicated. There is, as it were, a conspiracy to keep strong feelings below the surface, behind the facade of an institutional regime. Stereotyped phrases replace spontaneous communications, for adults and children alike.

There are often very dangerous subcultures in such places, but these are deeply hidden; collusive anxiety keeps them in the dark recesses.

I would suppose that systems of discipline in a place have a connection with the stress level which can be tolerated by the staff: the lower the level of stress toleration, the harsher the discipline. Organized and consistent (or rigid) methods of punishment, for example, tend to bypass conscious stress in the person who inflicts the punishment. Where there is 'punishment made to fit the crime' stress can easily be denied in a place. If a grown-up hits a child in a moment of anger, there is no escape from acceptance of some responsibility for both the action and the stress which led up to the action. This stress can be communicated to the chi'.'. Both grown-ups and children can gain from such experience, provided both are able to communicate their feelings to each other: because of the necessary insight involved, it is unlikely that such an episode will often be repeated. A person imposing disciplinary measures, however, often acts under considerable and complex stress of which he may not be aware. Both punisher and punished can be involved in a kind of unconscious excitement, which can result in a pairing set-up, and this may perpetuate a pathological punishing/punished pattern.

Professor Anthony in 'Group therapeutic techniques for residential units'[1] writes: 'The child very soon comes to know who wants to beat it and does not, who wants to treat it and cannot, and who imagines that he is treating it by beating it. The beaten child is learning slowly inside himself to become a beater.'

Psychotic children often turn out to be those who, because of having to endure intolerable and unthinkable stress, have withdrawn to a position in which they are able to believe that they

[1]Reprinted in Papers on Residential Work, Vol. 2 *Disturbed Children*, ed. R. Tod, 1968 p. 106

will never have to feel again. They may actually not feel stress, unless someone or something has broken through their massive defences.

Severely deprived babies often do not display overt indications of stress. They do not cry or rage, but remain passive and silent. Hospitalized children can be reduced fairly quickly to the same state.[1]

People working in this kind of setting tend to be so defended against awareness of their own and others' stress that they do not really come into close contact with the children, nor with each other in relation to the children. We could say that a great deal of deprivation goes unrecognized because children have either lost or been forbidden the relief of communicating stress in a direct way; and this is often because the adult cannot stand the guilt involved in knowing the harm that has been and continues to be done.

One of the important areas in which symbolic communication of stress can take place is that of play: in fact children often deal with stress through play. When institutionalized children are concerned, there is no symbolic play; they cannot symbolize what they have not experienced (this applies to all really deprived children).

I hope that what I have said concerning the need for everyone to be able to communicate stress does not suggest that I am recommending masochistic orgies. Nothing could be further from my thoughts. I have already said that the level of stress tolerance varies from person to person. Many people—grown-ups and children—can contain considerable stress within themselves without difficulty. One has no right, I think, to invade the privacy of such people, who will be conscious of stress but able to deal with the problem themselves. What I *am* saying is that, if stress is above this safe level, there needs to be direct communication and sympathetic response. If such an exchange is acceptable in a group of people working with disturbed children, there are likely to be fewer headaches for grown-ups and fewer broken windows for children!

[1] James Robertson, *A two-year old boy goes to hospital,* Tavistock Child Development Research Unit, 1953.

Now and then someone turns up in a residential place who seems to thrive on stress. Usually one finds that this sort of person organizes stressful situations because he is, in a way, addicted to stress. I do not feel that such a person should be encouraged to communicate stress, but rather to work in some other field where the fulfilling of this compulsive need will not be so likely to damage others.

Ideally, we all would be able consciously to contain stress within ourselves up to a high level, understanding the causes— whether simple or complex – and not needing to defend ourselves against insight. Actually, however, because we are real people we cannot do this beyond a certain point; at which something must happen. It is not easy to recognize this danger point, so that often we defend ourselves against stress before we become conscious of feelings which may be surging up from very deep within us.

Rage or terror are likely to surface in a fairly recognizable form; but envy (about which Klein has taught us so much) can produce agonizing stress and yet remain unconscious. Even if we are conscious of envy this is a difficult form of stress to communicate, because nobody wants to acknowledge the feelings of inadequacy which envy implies.

Some time ago a skilled and experienced therapist worked for a year with us at the Bush: I shall refer to her as Emily. Emily was deeply involved with a difficult boy of ten called Paul. These two were going through a phase of Paul's treatment during which he was regressed to babyhood in relation to Emily. This regression was localized: Emily made special symbolic adaptations to his needs (such as Sechehaye describes), and in all sorts of ways was giving him primary experience which had been missing during the first year of his life. Emily was under a simple but continuous kind of stress which she could tolerate; she had the support and concern of the other members of the team who knew how important this regressed phase must be to child and therapist and who gave support to their therapeutic involvement.

Paul's mother had a new baby which she wanted to show to Paul, so Emily took him to see his home many miles away on a cold winter's day with an icy wind blowing down the streets of the slum in which he lived. Paul's mother was always maternally preoccupied with her babies during the first months of their lives;

as they began to separate out from her into people in their own right she rejected her children, they were no longer part of her. This is what had happened to Paul when he was a small baby, as soon as he was weaned.

Paul's mother welcomed Paul and Emily, but in a preoccupied way. She brought in the baby to show her son, and then fed it at her breast. From that moment onwards she seemed to cease to be aware of their presence, so absorbed was she with her baby. Eventually Emily said that they must go: Paul's mother, suddenly noticing her, exclaimed 'But it is very cold, you are not warmly enough dressed – I will lend you my coat!' In a daze, Emily accepted the coat, and she and Paul set out on the journey back to the Bush. She did not tell us what had happened until later: Paul seemed quite happy, Emily very tired, but next day she was ill with a fever, and most distressed. At first she could not bear to think or talk about what had caused her so much anguish; but as she gradually described the whole experience to me, we could see that she was in an acute stress, complicated by envy.

You will remember that Emily was maternally preoccupied with Paul in a conscious and therapeutic way. The experience she and the boy were going through together was illusionary (although really felt), but the mother/baby unity of Paul's mother and her new baby was real objectively and subjectively. Emily, therefore, who was essentially a maternal person, was suddenly attacked by desperate envy of motherhood. The therapist and patient in the course of provision of a regression were faced by the mother and baby in the midst of original primary experience.

Emily was not conscious at the time of feeling envy: she could remember being intensely cold (physically), neither in touch with Paul nor with the mother and baby, she felt isolated and excluded. When Paul's mother pitied her (I think that the mother's action was not motivated by *compassion*), offering Emily her coat, it was as though she was regarding Emily as a poor creature to whom she could give kindness; in this way she denied the value of the help which Emily was giving to her son Paul. Paul's role in all this was a further complicating factor. He seemed to have been projectively identified with the baby at his mother's breast; a projection which, of course, broke the slender thread of his link with Emily, intensifying her feelings of isolation and inadequacy.

The stress caused by Emily's unconscious envy had not been realized or communicated in time to prevent a breakdown into psychosomatic illness. Following her gain of insight and her communication to me, she could tolerate her envy, and made a rapid recovery from her illness. It is easy to see how intolerable it must have been for Emily to feel envy of the very person whom she felt to be responsible for her patient's deprivation.

The leader of a treatment team, be he head, principal, director, or warden, has to be sensitively tuned-in to evidence of stress among his team and among the children in his care. He needs sufficient courage and integrity on occasions to communicate his own stress to his team. John Armstrong, the Headmaster of the Mulberry Bush School, talked to an audience of people who work in special schools; he described some incident, finishing: 'And I looked at this child with hate, and he returned my look of hate. We both knew that we hated each other.' The troubled chairman asked John whether he was sure that he had really felt hate. John assured her that his was so. His audience was grateful to him, and rightly so; they accepted an important communication.

Liz Greenway, at that time a member of the team, was talking to Ronnie (aged eight). Ronnie said to her, in sugary tones, 'You're so kind to me, Liz.' Liz replied, 'But I lose my temper with you, Ronnie, and you lose yours with me.' He could accept this correction of the sentimentality that is really denied hate: because Liz could stand reality, however awful, he could also.

It is important that anyone who is feeling persecuted, badly treated, overlooked, or devalued, should be able to talk about these feelings to someone who can respond without collusion. Often there may be an objectively real grievance somewhere; but in any case, however irrational such feelings may be they are terribly *real* to the persecuted one—be it grown-up or child. Just to be able to surface such feelings can sometimes make insight possible, so that the sufferer can sort out reality from projection (projection makes such stress complex). If a child says to me, 'No one likes me, everyone is on to me', I would be likely to say, 'How awful you must be feeling', because it is the *feeling* he is talking about and this is real. I think one can neither usefully argue nor reassure on these occasions. A grown-up, however, who constantly feels persecuted is at risk in working with disturbed children; the kind of person who can say with James Payn (1884):

> I had never had a piece of toast
> Particularly long and wide
> But fell upon the sanded floor,
> And always on the buttered side.

I have written in this paper for the most part about individuals communicating stress, directly or indirectly. I shall now turn finally to group intercommunication under stress.

Miller, writing in 1960 about the use of small groups for staff training in the penal system, stated: 'Thus psychologically untrained staff are constantly exposed to the psychological stress of being in interpersonal situations with highly disturbed human beings.' Individuals under this strain naturally bring their stress into group situations. I have for a long time been concerned with the problem of enabling workers to include their own feelings in reporting and group discussion. I started to wonder about 'the situation' in residential treatment as comparable to 'the session' in psychotherapy. I thought that 'the situation' needed to involve experience between the reporting adult and a child or children: an experience which was felt, recognized and realized, and communicable to others.

This idea gradually evolved into what I have called 'context profiles', a kind of reporting which makes use of experience (rather than observations) between staff and child in the course of a week, at all times of the day and night.[1] Clare Winnicott, in 'Communicating with children',[2] writes: 'Shared experiences are perhaps the only non-threatening form of communication which exists.' I feel that *reporting* on shared experience can also be fairly non-threatening in an undefended group.

Here I am only going to consider a fragment of a group discussion following the accumulation and recording of such a context profile, which had already been read by the team. I think this is an interesting discussion. Matters to be considered are: the stress involved; rivalry between the various people helping

---

[1] Papers on Residential Work, Vol. 3 *Therapy in Child Care*, chap. 10.
[2] Papers on Residential Work, Vol. 2 *Disturbed Children*, chap. 7.

this child; feelings of inadequacy and guilt in respect of the limited amount that we have been able to do with this very ill boy; frustration in regard to his capacity for group disruption – anger and disappointment; envy in regard to earlier workers (with whom present workers may be unfavourably compared). Because the team are individually and collectively acutely aware of such stress factors, their communication is not hampered or stereotyped.

David had been in the children's department of a mental hospital before he came to us, as one of the most deprived children I have met. He was at that time unintegrated in most areas. There was a very frail ego (built on such good experience as had come his way in babyhood and early childhood). In a few areas, therefore, he could function; for the rest, he was chaotic, needing almost total emotional containment. I think our discussion will explain more about him.

John: What I could not help but notice in reading all this was the lack of involvement with David which there seems to be: some of the notes I put in were really to indicate what David is doing now and what he is not doing, compared with a year or so ago.

Myself: Wouldn't you say that possibly this is because David is a running concern—you know, that he has a kind of outfit? This certainly seemed to me to come out in my session with him today. I seem to find this also in the material. To me there is the David who is tough, the bully, who attacks, who goes for people; and there is also the David who plays the recorder really beautifully. He played it to me this afternoon—he asked in the session if he could play it to me– and it was most moving: the delicacy of his fingers, the way in which he holds the recorder.

The contrast between this and the way in which he normally uses his fingers is tremendous. I feel there are these two aspects of David which, in a way, shut him off from the other people a bit, unless one can contact the part of him which plays the recorder. That's why one is in difficulties about getting close to him.

John: In a way I don't know how it has struck other people, but it seems to me that in the last fortnight the outward David is not what we have had. There has not been nearly so much beating up and sly kicking. How much all this has got to do with the recorder I don't know.

Myself: Well really the recorder is just a symbol. .... I am just using the recorder as one aspect of his personality.

Hans: There is an apparent transition to a next stage, quite consciously over a long time. I feel I've had a long period making a primary provision. The fact that he came to me was more because he was making an attempt now into entering a suitable course of work.

Myself: Or secondary experience?

Hans: Yes. And as far as *I* have observed I think it has happened.

Myself: May I interrupt just a minute? There is Liz, and before her there was Faith, and one or two people in between . . .

John: Tita and Gillah briefly in between . . .

Myself: Yes, that's right. So that in fact there has been a sort of chain of mother figures that really now must be fairly strong and . . .

Liz: Mothers?

Myself: Yes indeed, mothers.

Liz: You may remember it was where I spoke of David preparing to leave my group to go over to that of a man, and making tentative approaches, looking for a father figure. He tried to make some connection with Hans in a magical sort of way. I have noticed how magic or apparent magic and power mattered so much to him, as if to make up for inadequacies in my maternal provision.

Myself: This makes very interesting sense of his recorder, doesn't it? As one could suppose that the making of music is a kind of symbolization of the early experience with you.

Liz: He wanted me to get him a transistor. And he wanted me to teach him to play the recorder. I was unable to teach him because I knew nothing of playing the recorder, and Hans was able to help him. My failure here was important.

Myself: This gives one the maternal history, so that learning lessons and so on are based on a masculine identification: learning the recorder has go to do with fathers.

Liz: But you will remember where I said that David has told me his father was Greek; that I would not be able to spell his

17

name, that I would not be able to write it in Greek and so on.

Myself: One wonders what Greek means to David, if it has a real significance.

Liz: And he was asking how many words one could make from his surname, and about when he was born.

Myself: Apropos of his being born. Today at the very end of the session I was reminding him of how he talked to me about his birth (I met him in the very early days at the Limes[1]–I was trying to work out just how long ago this was) and how he described to me that he had been dropped in fact from an aeroplane on to bare ground, and had lain there till his mother found him.

John: I think his father was an airman.

Myself: That fits, doesn't it? . . . there he was on the hard bare ground and suddenly his mother came along . . . he says he remembers being found. Extraordinary, isn't it? It is relevant here to what happened in the session. He said that he would like to play squiggles–I couldn't remember if he was a squiggle child–however, he said that we had played squiggles.[2] There were three squiggles in this particular game, but I shall only describe two. David turned my squiggle into a large tangled sort of bow: then suddenly, down in the corner of the paper, he drew a rather beautiful form, a little like a tudor rose or a medallion–very small and precise. David said: 'That's a big bow, but this is what I really wanted to make.' I said cautiously that it looked to be more like a flower, but he didn't take it up. I was thinking really that here was this great big thing which he called a bow, but which looked to me very like a knot, and down here was this very small, neat, collected little thing which I thought was terribly important. I thought again here of the two aspects of David, and here they were: but I didn't say so.

David described the third squiggle: 'There are two planes signalling, one close and one far away.' I said I wondered what they were signalling to each other, and David said he didn't

---

[1] The Limes is a staff house.

[2] 'Squiggles' is a technique which I use with children, in which I make a small squiggle on a piece of paper, the child turns the squiggle into anything he likes. and we discuss the result.

know. I said I wondered why it was important, and David said: 'Well, they are both signalling to each other–I don't know what about.' I asked: 'Do they understand each other? This is the important thing–that they should understand one another–then it doesn't matter that other people do not know what it is about.' A discussion followed in which I made suggestions based on this and on the second squiggle, that these were (or could be) two parts of him. So he said: 'What nonsense! There is only one of me, you can see I am one.' I answered that I did see, but I didn't know if I could feel like David about him. So then we talked about this and he said: 'What do you mean?' I talked about the bully, boss part of him and all that, and he said was I sure I wasn't thinking about Tom. So I said I really was quite sure that I was thinking about David. He was extremely resistant, at first taking the line that anybody could see that there was only one of him: I agreed that this was all that could be seen, but I did feel there were two different parts of David as a person. He disagreed, and then I asked whether the part of him that is bossy knew about the part of him for whom Faith used to make custard. He said at once, 'No', and I suggested that this could be confirmatory evidence that the two parts of him were out of touch with each other. There is the part of him that plays the recorder and there is also the part of him that Faith used to make custard for ... We talked about the recorder and the custard; this being a way of talking about parts of him. I said: 'Does this still sound nonsense to you, or does it make any kind of sense?' And he said, no, it didn't sound like nonsense to him, he was thinking about it. I said that if this was so, perhaps one could imagine that the tough bullying part was really protecting the little real part– I said that the recorder part seemed to be the real part.

I saw a great change in the description of what he had done with the recorder, and it did seem to me to confirm very much the fact that he is trying to give his real self a voice.

John: There is the fact that he would time after time go away to the sitting room and play.

Myself: There are lots of descriptions all through the context profile: the recorder is the clue to this boy.

Brian: This recorder: at times when he is threatened, say by Tom,

19

he uses it in a way as a snake charmer would charm a snake. But of course, it does not have this effect. It is fascinating, he is not looking at the recorder, he is looking at the boy.

Hans: Of course I knew that David had started the recorder with Royston. When he came into my group he wanted me to continue because he knew I could, but I refused because I felt in this case it was too important–though occasionally he would ask me something to do with his music. I think it is a good sign that he is able to keep a rapport with a special person.

Myself: Yes, it is also conscious, and you will have to consider this in thinking about his establishing a father; he is building up his father from a selection of people: as he has also in a way built up a mother from a selection of people. The way things have worked out, this is how he is able to do it. The amazing thing is the amount he has achieved because of the group of people trying to work in the same way and doing the same things for him. He has shown me–and this is very interesting– he has shown me the other recorder: he got it out of the drawer. I asked: 'Is that all right, do you think?' and he said, 'Oh yes, just to show you and then put it back, that's all right–you tell Roy.' I said that I would. So he took it out of the drawer and showed it to me. He said: 'It's beautiful, quite beautiful. But it has got to get moist quite gradually. It would be awful if it just became what is called a "hoarse" recorder. This wouldn't make a nice sound–it would be loud and horrible.' I thought to myself–I didn't say this–just like David's voice when he is tough and horrible.

I felt there were two voices, and the recorder really was the voice of the real David . . . the David struggling to grow.

Liz: Do you remember how sensitive he was to voice, and he got so annoyed when I tried to read a story to the group with expression. He would say 'Read it in your own voice.'

Even in this fragment of a context, there is evidence that the speakers have dealt, and are dealing, with considerable stress.

1. At the beginning John drew attention to the lack of involvement with David, who has been with us for several years. John and all of us had felt guilt and anxiety about this fact, but neither John nor any of us denied the realization in order to

attempt to preserve an emotional equilibrium.

2. Hans told us that he had to provide David with primary experience when he first joined Hans's group. He pointed out that this provision was not completed in Liz's group, but that now David is able to go on to secondary experience. Hans had long since dealt with conscious resentment in regard to providing for someone who was so out of step with the rest of his relatively integrated group.

3. Liz was able to speak of inadequacies in her maternal provision, instead of blaming someone else or denying her failure. She went on to show that her failure in connection with David's learning the recorder could in fact be used by David. She could tell us that Hans was able to offer David something that she could not. A little later she speaks of David pointing out her deficiencies. All this could have been denied or projected, and be simmering under the surface.

4. I felt guilty and unhappy about David, because I had worked with him quite a lot when he first came to us. For various reasons I had lost touch with him. Now I felt a need to link past and present both in my own work and that of the others. In talking with David and the team I felt better as I realized just how much other people had achieved.

5. Hans, a very musical person, left the teaching of David's recorder to Royston, outside the group. This cannot have been emotionally easy to do; but he was concerned as we all were with the primary task of helping David. (We tend to work in terms of main and supplementary roles.)

6. Liz, at the end, mentioned that David liked her to read 'in her own voice'. This is the sort of wounding thing that disturbed children say, which can easily be felt as an attack on the worker. Liz did not make this mistake; she could tolerate the pain of being criticized or despised by a child.

7. We were all able, at different points during the whole discussion, to refer to earlier members of the treatment team who had helped David. Such reference is always emotionally loaded, because we are all having to accept the idealization by children of workers who have left; while we ourselves are angry with these people for going away. The fact that we know we are angry and have talked about our feelings frees us to value what

they have done and to miss them.

I have attempted in this paper to consider some of the many problems arising in the communication of stress.

I think we must accept that in the course of the residential treatment of severely disturbed children we are bound to encounter more and higher degrees of stress than would otherwise be likely to come our way. There will be times when the level of this stress will be higher than can be tolerated and contained. I consider that there will be less harm caused to ourselves and others if such intolerable stress can be communicated, rather than hidden or disguised. This communication cannot take place except among people who can acknowledge stress in themselves and are consequently able to be undefended and in empathy with others.

2

Emotionally deprived parents, 1969

The therapeutic management of emotionally deprived parents
whose children are in residential treatment

*I have always of necessity and of choice worked with the parents of disturbed
children. This particular paper was written for a course run by Chris
Holtom at Bristol University for child care officers, probation officers,
and others. My audience gave many interesting examples of experiences
with deprived parents.*

I am finding difficulty in starting to write this paper, because I
cannot decide where to establish a beginning. I am going to make
basic assumptions concerning *your* starting point: I am going
to assume that most of what I might say has already been experienced, realized and conceptualized by all of us, so that I could
be wasting our time in covering a well tilled field.

There is a considerable collection of literature on the whole
subject of separation of children from their families, with which
I am sure you are already familiar; so that I propose to narrow
down the subject to certain special considerations which could
perhaps be interesting to discuss together.

We are all one way or another concerned with the effects of
severe emotional deprivation in parents and children, and with the
phenomena of 'acting out' which stem from a breakdown in
communication. At a time of crisis—such as can lead to the placement of a child away from his family—emotional deprivation (if
present to any extent in the child or the parents) can lead to violent
acting out, through breakdown in communication both with the
self and others.

The people in a residential place, be it approved school, maladjusted children's school or children's home, may be suddenly
confronted with a massive bloc of deprivation; which can have
serious effects on grown ups and children alike. How best we

can deal with this confrontation is what I wish to consider here.

In the therapeutic school where I work, we are selecting cases entirely on a basis of severe emotional deprivation during the first year of life. This being so, we have had to evolve a plan for admission which will avoid a sudden and tremendous build up of stress for ourselves, the parents, and the child.

Because children are referred to us from child guidance clinics, we are in a position to make the whole process of separation from the family and admission to the school fairly gradual. We start with interviews at the clinic, followed by one or more visits to the school. Eventually the parents bring the child to the actual placement, to people and a place already fairly familiar. There have, however, been occasions when we have admitted an urgent case from one moment to the next. I am sure that such a course of action is traumatic, but must become necessary in many cases where a child is committed to an approved school, or has suddenly to be taken into care because of some family catastrophe. On the whole, our small customers at the Mulberry Bush have been living in a state of endemic crisis, without total breakdown having taken place. Home, therefore, however pathological, continues to exist, thus making a gradual process of placement possible. Because deprived children tend to be the children of deprived parents, we can assume an absence of transitional experience in their lives: the filling of gaps in their emotional experience must be our primary task, and 'bridging' techniques in placement procedure can make a foundation on which we can hope to build, in providing primary experience.

The sudden removal of a child from his family, however pathological, is likely to be traumatic, and to reproduce previous traumatic breaks in the continuity of the child's existence which have led to his present state. Nothing can be more likely and more traumatic than such faithful reproduction for child and parents of earlier disasters, in the residential setting. There are circumstances in which there is no alternative, where transitional techniques cannot be employed, and the break between child and family has to take place from one moment to the next: at least we can be aware that this is something terrible, even in cases where there may be cruelty and neglect.

It is important to realize that the parents of severely emotionally deprived children are likely to be themselves deprived, even though this may not be immediately apparent from histories or initial interviews. One is liable to expect envy and hostility from the parents of disturbed children, arising from their feelings of inadequacy in having to allow outsiders to care for their children. This kind of reaction is certainly to be expected from the parents of neurotic children: in cases of deprivation the problem is rather different. Parents in such cases feel envy also, but they are envious not of us, but *of their own children*, because their children are receiving the care which they know themselves to need. Once we become aware of this particular form of envy, we are already in a position to establish a link with the child *and* his parents (as compared with casework with individuals). It is possible to make limited provision for deprived parents, in terms of communication, food, time, and so on.

We are going to have a difficult task, in any case, in attempting to preserve the child's place in the family. If we start our programme by breaking the continuity of the family life by a *sudden act of separation*, we are certain to have much more difficulty than we need expect. If we can link both parents and child to us and the place, by localized provision before the child is actually placed, we may be able to replace an *act* of separation by a *process*; which, though sad and painful, need not be inevitably traumatic and can establish a bridge between family and place. Psychiatric social workers, health visitors, child care officers, teachers and probation officers can all play a part in this process, by acting as catalysts through whom the child and his family can come into communication with the people in the place (be it children's home, school for maladjusted children, or approved school). This assumes that the main catalyst agent is already in touch with the people in the residential place: this would seem to be essential in any case.

Deprived people, both grown-ups and children, have usually had to shift their trust from people to things: environment, therefore, can offer either security or threat. The unknown environment tends to be the threatening one, and I have known deprived parents and children to disorientate completely in going round our school for the first time. One must provide families with a base, a 'safe place' from which to explore the strange milieu. This base needs, I think, to be a sitting room of some kind, in which they can talk with members of staff, where they can have some food, and where they can be securely alone.

The illusionary 'safe place' will be a permanent need, because such people have no safe place within themselves. The 'safe place' can only exist at the price of other places being 'dangerous': if the safe place becomes less safe, the other places become more dangerous.

Initially, we ourselves combined with our residential environment will be felt as a dangerous place; so that by providing a family base we are preventing the child's family from starting their contact with us from a persecuted position. Of course we are hoping to establish relationships, but this is a long-term treatment aim. In working with deprived families, 'things' may come before 'people', just as acting-out is likely to precede communication.

What we *do* can in a symbolic way perhaps be more use than what we *say*, however relevant the latter may be. However warm a welcome we give to the family, what we feel and what we express may not reach them if the sun is not shining or if the room is cold. The hot cups of tea may convey this warmth, evoking what Sechchaye has described as symbolic realization.

When we are trying to help neurotic people, we can assume that they will transfer this and that on to us from their own early experiences; so we may become established in all sorts of roles which do not often have much to do with what we really are like as real people. We accept such roles, but do not act out *in* the roles; we keep these within the framework of our particular functions.

Working with deprived parents and children, we may be having very different responsibilities and commitments, since for them there can be no transference in areas where they have not had experience. This state of affairs leads to what Little has called 'delusional transference': for deprived people we *are* the parents— there is no 'as if' in such a feeling. It is all very well when such a delusional transference is positive, but when the negative form turns up, we can feel destroyed by the violence of annihilating rage which we may collect. Sometimes we may receive this terrible onslaught in the first place; more often we start with a positive delusional transference, in which we are the ideal parents who can take care at last of the parents *and* their children. They have been looking for such maternal care all their lives: so that if we reject these deprived fathers and mothers of deprived children, we confirm all that they suppose. On the other hand, we are in no position to take on full therapeutic responsibilities in relation to these families: it is their *children* who are our clients. Workers in a residential place recognize intuitively the needs of deprived parents, and realize how overwhelming would be their demands: so they tend to defend themselves against intolerable commitment, and in doing so tend to build a wall between themselves and the family of the child, who is now on the worker's side of the wall of defence.

What I am suggesting is the possibility of meeting the parents' needs in a highly localized way from the start. In fact we are much more likely to be able to give real therapeutic care to deprived parents than to neurotic ones, because *provision* rather than interpretation is the primary need. It is this fact that makes it possible for unanalysed therapists to learn this very special skill. The workers will need support and supervision; but they are quite likely to have sufficient personal resources at their disposal to provide appropriate therapeutic management in all areas for the deprived children, and in localized form for their parents.

People working with deprived parents tend to ask: 'How can we hope to help such damaged people?—how can the little we can do be of any use?' I think we can only reply as we would to the same question put to us concerning severely emotionally deprived children and adolescents: 'The ego is built of experiences. Therefore, in terms of strengthening a weak ego, we can be sure that no positive experience that we provide will be wasted.' This is a problem of economy, not of success or failure. We can only give what can be spared; but localized provision can be of value: parents and children can increase functioning areas through such provision.

I very rarely use the word 'adult', preferring to say 'grown-up'. 'Adult' seems to deny that *a child has grown up,* confirming the split which many parents and children feel divides them from each other. In recognizing the deprived child who has grown up into this unhappy and troubled parent, we can understand the unsatisfied and continued childhood needs of such a grown-up.

Talking about herself, a little patient of mine once said of her drawing 'This is a puddle in a pond'. The child hidden in the personality of the grown-up may be as secret as the puddle in the pond. The more well a mother is, the more linked she is with her own childhood, and therefore the more able to identify with her child's needs. If we can help the deprived grown-up to let us know about the hidden child with its desperate needs and to allow us to meet some of them (however small), we may be putting the mother in a position to feel for her child.

Of course, this is equally true of fathers, but because deep deprivation belongs to the first year of life we can assume that the mother is our first consideration, in the interests of her child. On occasions, however, the father has been the parent who has been able to feel maternal towards the baby, while the mother has been forced into a paternal role. Pathological though this is, we may have to be thankful that there is maternal feeling somewhere, and make use of what is available. In such a case we certainly cannot begin to alter the psychopathology of the parents. Here again, we must accept a very limited aim, but the little we *can* do may go a long way eventually.

It is a delicate task to help the deprived children in the personalities of the parents, whilst continuing to respect them as grown-ups, objectively speaking. However, we do respect as people within their own right the patients we are treating who are indeed *actually* children: similarly, we can soon perceive the functioning areas in even very deprived parents, where we can respect and support their maturity.

I remember, from long ago, a very disturbed father whose child was having a period of treatment in the Mulberry Bush School. We had come to know him quite well, and he was talking about his own need to come and be a child also in our care. He said, 'I wish I could do something here that I would do if I were small and living here.' I knew that he could draw very well, and suggested that he might paint a picture on a wall in the place. He was tremendously pleased, set to work sitting on the floor in the corner of a play room, and painted a fine ship—low down on the wall, at just about the height he would have been able to reach as a little boy. We could all (grown-ups and children alike) respect and admire his skill and the beauty of the ship; but at the same time we could sympathize with the child who was briefly among the other children in our care.

I have considered some ways by which parents may be linked to their residentially placed children, through their own localized experiences provided by the people in the residential place. I wish now to consider the more direct links between the deprived child placed residentially, and his parents.

Communication between the deprived child and his parents has probably broken down–if it has ever existed. There can, of course, be an institutionalized exchange of stereotyped phrases, but this is not real communication. The parents will react violently to the child's acting out, but are most unlikely to see this as attempted communication; indeed, they are liable to *re*act out themselves. We tend to think in terms of *maintaining* a link between child and home: but in the care of deprived family constellations, our task may well be to establish a link for the first time.

The telephone can be very useful: often this will be the first occasion on which child and parents have spoken to each other by telephone, and the very newness of the situation can break through the stereotyped conversation and lead to real communication. We explain to parents during initial interviews that we do not censor telephone calls or letters; so that (we point out) at first the child is likely to use this freedom to complain about us and other children. The deprived child will have learnt that his best chance of contacting his parents has been on a basis of persecution. This is the area where his parents can projectively identify with him, because they themselves will be paranoid in a very primitive way. If we can show children and parents that we can allow them to verbalize such complaints (which are often wholly irrational) without being hostile or punitive, we shall be making a start in the clearing of ground for communication in the family.

We have noted how often a child will hurt himself, or develop psychosomatic symptoms, or get himself attacked, just before the start of holidays. He is trying in his way to ensure a place for himself in the family to which he is returning and from which he has been excluded. He feels–usually correctly–that a persecuted niche is the only one on which he can count in his home, better this than nothing. Gradually we may be able to alter this dreadful pattern: sometimes this can be done by helping the child to bring back home something from the place–a bunch of flowers, a cake he has baked, or a stool he has made.

Both child and parents will be constantly threatened by a harsh projected super-ego: all authority will seem threatening and punitive to them. We are, for them, authority figures. They may adapt to our demands, but this will be placating and based on fear. When we try to meet their needs and care for them, we do not cease to be authority figures; but we can replace the harsh super-ego by a benign one. Of course we should like to be in ego-supporting roles, but for this to be possible there must be egos to support! Working with really deprived people (whether parents or children) we must learn to do without functioning egos in our clients: bits of ego there will be, but not enough.

We have been perhaps too willing, in the past, to decry the super-ego (the conscience arousing guilt and anxiety). The concept of the benign super-ego has not been so familiar. The acceptance of a parental authority role based on compassion and concern involves us in a different kind of involvement from the supportive role which is appropriate for work with integrated neurotic clients.

I recently had an initial interview in a child guidance clinic with the little son (aged eight) of psychotic parents: he was in care under Section I.[1] I shall refer to him here as Tommy. Both his parents could just about survive in society, but Tommy, a charming and intelligent boy, was breaking under the strain of widly inconsistent and unreliable management (he ran away from any placement, and from home). Discussing his problems with the psychiatrist, I gave it as my view that Tommy must be brought before a court as beyond parental control, so that he could be sent to us with legal controls. I suggested that if this plan could be accepted by Tommy and his parents, they might all feel more secure. Otherwise, I was sure, Tommy would be whisked away from us on impulse—either his own, or that of his parents. I wanted to establish authority between impulse and action. Accordingly, since the psychiatrist agreed with this line of thought, we discussed our ideas with the child and then with the mother; explaining our reasons, but in such a way that they were able to accept such authority, which was not felt by them as punitive (we have still

---

[1]Children Act 1948 (Section 1 makes provision for local authorities to receive children into care on a voluntary basis).

to learn the father's views).

I can remember several cases in which the children in treatment with us were making good progress, and we seemed to have a reasonably good contact with the mothers, albeit of a rather superficial kind. The fathers, however, stayed as shadowy figures in the background, both in regard to ourselves and to the clinics concerned: they appeared to accept what was being done to help their children, they did not participate but neither did they interfere. Suddenly, however, these fathers announced that their children must now come home. Nothing that any of us could do or say influenced this decision, and these children left us long before their treatment was completed.

However difficult the task of looking after these very disturbed people (be they grown-ups or children), their individual needs must somehow be met in very different ways. I think perhaps one's own attitude can make this easier. If one is working in a personal way rather than in an institutional way, the treatment approach can be flexible. If there is not too rigid an organization (in regard to visiting, for example) then there is not so much likelihood that the social structure will be disrupted by individual plans for parents' visits.

I remember a very ill mother, whom I met for the first time with her little daughter (aged seven) in a hospital department. The mother had tried to kill herself and her child, whom I shall call Polly. The hospital had offered to be responsible for both till other arrangements could be made—an offer which the court had accepted. There was a symbiotic tie of a most primitive kind between mother and child. I played squiggles with both of them together in their small bedroom, but I forget the exact details of this game. The mother was sure that she and Polly could not be separated, but she agreed, following a long discussion, to come and see the Mulberry Bush, brought by the psychiatric social worker. During this visit we played squiggles again; and between the two of them, mother and child produced from my squiggle a chicken coming out of an egg.

Polly came to us on condition that her mother could visit or telephone her at any time. Presently her mother started to tell me about her own life, and for the first time wanted to see me apart from Polly. I suggested that on these occasions we should meet alone in Oxford, to be joined later by Polly. In the Botanical Gardens we met on warm spring days, during which Polly's mother started to attack me – only with her voice – but in such a terrible way that I felt destroyed by her. I was often tempted to withdraw from the full blast of psychotic rage (the other face of her suicide attempt): but not to survive her 'destruction' of me would have been to take a terrible revenge upon her.

So our meetings continued, until one day she was telling me how vile we all were and how awful it was for her to have to leave Polly in our care, and that she had been forced by us to do so. I pointed out that there was no reason why she should have to leave her child with us – there were other schools – would she prefer us to make arrangements for Polly to go elsewhere? I held my breath at this point, but Polly's mother, having sat in silence for a moment, said slowly: 'She'd better stay at the Bush. There wouldn't be someone I could shout at, like I do at you, if she went somewhere else. Sensible people wouldn't stand for it!' On this basis Polly's treatment could continue, although eventually her mother removed her on an impulse.

What I am saying about deprived parents of children in treatment is that we cannot count on their evolvement. We may well have to accept them exactly as they are, have been and will be all their lives. We can nevertheless so gear our treatment programme as to make it possible to include them with their children in what we plan: should we fail to do so, they will certainly break into their children's treatment because of envy and feelings of rejection.

While a deprived child is in our care, we may ourselves be helping him to establish a place in his family *for the first time*. A neurotic child may be a square peg trying to fit into a round hole: a deprived child may have to evolve into a peg for whom we have to carve a hole – this can only be done on a basis of caring for the family as well as the child.

3
Integration and
unintegration, 1969

*This paper was written before chapter 5, 'Meeting children's emotional
needs in residential work', so much that I have said here is contained in the
later paper. However, I am including this short piece here because this is
where I first stated my realization of the urgent need for classification in
residential places.*

I have felt for some time that the difficulty which most bedevils
the residential treatment of disturbed and emotionally deprived
children is the mixture of integrated and unintegrated in any one
unit. The presence of such a mixture puts a terrifying strain on
both staff and children, resulting in violent reactions.

The cornerstone of the ideas I am considering is this: I am sure
that there is an enormous problem of *incompatibility*, with which
integrated and unintegrated children are burdened if they are
living together, and that this problem puts too heavy a load on
staff. Those children who have not been able to establish a more
or less functioning self are deeply threatened when confronted
by functioning in others. They react to such a confrontation by
a primitive defence which can be termed disruption (Erikson has
applied this term to play). For example: if an unintegrated child
comes into a group of integrated children who are playing an
organized game, he will feel so threatened by the functioning
children, he will at once attempt to disrupt (disintegrate) the group.
The integrated children in the functioning group will become
so anxious in the face of often repeated disruption that they will
cease to make good use of their capacity to function and will, of
course, feel bitterly resentful towards the disruptive ones, and
towards the grown-ups who allow such disruption to take place.

The unintegrated children cannot stand functioning in others
unless it is directed towards provision for themselves: the integrated children cannot stand constant disruption of their functioning as individuals or in groups. This is one kind of gross

33

incompatibility which can make life impossible for both kinds of children.

One can argue, of course (and rightly), that there are areas of incompatibility in all relationships. These areas can be denied or avoided, they can be battlefields, or they can be acknowledged and respected as unalterable (as they often are). Now and then in ordinary life settings, love and insight can bridge the gulf between the incompatible areas of two grown ups; but this is an achievement, because the causes for such incompatibility are so deeply rooted in the nature of the self, and the way in which the self has been built: this need not point to a lack of integration. The kind of incompatibility which I am describing is basic, in that one group is a threat to the survival of the other.

Another aspect of the incompatibility of integrated and unintegrated children is the incidence of panic amongst the unintegrated ones. Anyone, however integrated, is liable to panic for brief instants now and then, but unintegrated children panic constantly when emotionally they are *in a gap within themselves*. Panic can appear as rage, fright or despair: it can result in violent acting out or total immobilization. The therapeutic treatment of panic involves holding, containment, and very intensive care from a deeply involved therapist. Nothing is more difficult than to treat panic in the middle of a normally functioning group–at a meal time, or in a class, or play group, for example.

In order to make a classification of children in terms of integration, in a residential place, these two factors – disruption and panic–may be used to give some indication of the position. Clearly, in an approved school or a school for maladjusted children, there will be many more unintegrated children to be found in the group. I believe, however, that there is a high proportion–higher than we realize–of unintegrated children in children's homes and reception centres. A recognition of the effect which this presence must have on more integrated children and the people working in the place is a first essential step towards improvement.

Of course panic and disruption are not the only characteristics of unintegrated children, but these are overt symptoms which are quite easy to recognize and are reliable indications of unintegrated states. Once such a classification has been made, we are faced with problems of management. Would it be better for unintegrated children to be grouped together in special units that provide primary experience, or can the basic incompatibility of the integrated and unintegrated be bypassed within the one unit with special provision for the two groups? One argument (amongst many which would suggest the need for special units for un-integrated children) is that in, for example, a children's home, there may well be many more integrated than unintegrated children present. This is certainly the impression which I have received from listening to workers. It would be difficult to make special provision for, say, three out of sixteen children; the inte-grated children could suffer; the staffing ratio would not allow the amount of time and care needed for the therapeutic manage-ment of three children in a group of sixteen. There may be child-ren's homes where there is a higher incidence of unintegrated children—perhaps six or seven in a group of sixteen: in such a case I would have thought that special management could be provided. Let us consider the possibilities in such a home. I am going to assume that all the children go out to school, and that the age range is from five to fifteen. The areas where special management could be needed would be meal times, bedtimes, the early mornings and play times. Bedtime always presents difficulties to unintegrated children, producing frequent panics, acting-out and disruptive activity, *unless* their needs are being met. Such children need to be cared for in the very special way I have described elsewhere:[1] for example, they need individually filled personal hotwater bottles (such a colour, so full, so hot—*this* bottle belonging to *this* child). They need special 'tucking in', and highly personal communication with the therapist worker con-cerned, once they are in bed. They may need a special kind of drink or sweet, their own cup, and so on.

Whilst it is possible to make such provision in a mixed group of integrated and unintegrated children, there are obvious dis-advantages in doing so. For example, this could invite integrated children to regress when they have no need. If all the children sleeping in one room are unintegrated, they will each have their

---

[1] See 'The problem of making adaptation to the needs of the individual child in a group' in Papers in Residential Work, Vol. 2, *Disturbed Children,* 1968.

own provision and will be as unconcerned by the presence of other children as babies would be. The integrated children would then be free to read, talk or go to sleep in a peaceful atmosphere, instead of being disturbed by the panics and disruption which can lead to such bitter resentment and retaliation. The staff would be in a position to meet needs in an appropriate way, rather than struggling through intolerable and unresolved difficulties which arise from a mixture of grossly incompatible groups.

Meal times are another area of difficulty, and here perhaps two or more tables could help both groups (with three or four children at each table), thus avoiding a mixture of groups. Food is an essential field for primary provision: such a plan could make special arrangements feasible for the unintegrated, and which the integrated children would not in fact want for themselves.

Some of you may have read my suggestions for two types of play group,[1] one type assuming ego functioning, while the other would provide containment and primitive satisfactions.

Although I have not suggested acting out as a factor for classification, I wish to consider this typical phenomenon of unintegration from the viewpoint of provision. Acting out can be assumed to have resulted from a breakdown in communication. The re-establishment of a field of communication is therefore an important therapeutic task. Here again, in a mixed discussion group there will be disruption and panic for obvious reasons. Separate groups of integrated and unintegrated children can, however, function successfully and can lead to communication replacing acting out as unintegrated children learn to contain and verbalize their feelings. During the early stages of such communication, a flow of persecuted accusations are to be expected and accepted: that is to say, the reality of the persecuted feelings – not the validity of the accusations – must be accepted. It is easy to be trapped into proving how unreal these accusations seem to be; but in proving the point the therapeutic benefit of such communication can be lost.

I believe that in all units these small discussion groups should exist, taking place in the same room at the same time each day. The integrated ones will, of course, make use of such an opportu-

---

[1] 'Play as therapy in child care', in *Therapy in Child Care*, ch. 11

nity in quite a different way, but they also need a chance to talk in this special setting.

Ideally, in a mixed unit of integrated and unintegrated children there should be two 'quiet rooms'; one intended for functioning children, where they could read, paint or play quiet games without constant threats of disruption, and the other providing containment for non-functioning children, with large boxes, cushions, soft toys, blankets, etc. One room could be termed 'the quiet room club', with elected members, while the other could be called a 'box room', or some such name, which would not stress the real purpose for this room; its purpose could then emerge naturally as children started to use the facilities offered.

So far I have only discussed the management of a mixed group (in terms of integration) within one unit. The other possibility for consideration is the setting up of small residential units, catering only for the needs of unintegrated children. (Such a plan could easily exist in a 'cottage homes' arrangement.) If these special units could be set up, a flexible system would need to operate, by which children could move in and out according to their needs. These special units would require a high staff ratio (one grown-up to two children), and the staff would receive special training. Within the Cotswold Community (where I work) such a unit has already been in existence for long enough for us to see how well such provision can be used. The presence of this unit provides a valuable safety-valve, in that a disruptive, panicking actor-out can be referred to the special unit without imposing feelings of guilt and inadequacy on to the referring unit. It is now common for boys to refer themselves to the special unit, where primary experience is provided by a skilled team who have learnt the theory and practice of this kind of therapy in less than two years. The Mulberry Bush School caters only for unintegrated children, aged from five to twelve years. Here the presence of a recovering group of more or less integrated children presents a problem which has not yet been fully resolved. These recovering children have, however, themselves received the therapy of primary provision, so that they do understand to some extent the problems of the unintegrated children in treatment. But there is also a need here for more insulation, for a barrier against stimuli, to protect the newly established selves.

The ideas which I have put forward are based on limited experience and are only intended to provide a brief outline.

I have now been working at the Cotswold Community in a consultative role for nearly two years.[1] In common with other consultants, I was asked by Richard Balbernie, the Principal of the Cotswold Community, to try to find out for myself in what way I could be of use in the place. This flexible approach made it possible for me to feel my way, taking time and working in terms of the current context. What I have written up to this point are the conclusions I have reached with some certainty, so far: they are for the most part based on weekly discussions with the teams of the individual houses with which I have been connected. At first I did some work with the boys themselves, but I have found that I can be of more use to them indirectly—that is to say, working through the teams which help the boys. Anyhow, one session per week was hopelessly inadequate, and I found that the only way in which a single hour of psychotherapy could be of use was if it could be used afterwards for discussion with staff (of course, with the permission of the boy himself). Where unintegrated children were concerned, I pooled my resources with those of the staff, in order to work out a therapeutic programme of provision of primary experience for the particular boy—where I was, then and there. When working with an integrated boy, my main aim was to deepen the channels of communication between the boy and the staff caring for him.

The setting up of the small internal unit (known as the Cottage), explicitly planned for the provision of primary experience, took less than a year to establish as a functioning entity within the community. The speed with which the Cottage team learnt this highly skilled task astonished me, and made me think again about training in this field of work: I certainly had not realized how quickly a group of people *could* learn, in action. Perhaps learning as a group has advantages. The Cottage team has certainly come through deep and painful experiences in the course of realization about themselves in relation to the boys: I think that the outcome has made the difficulties and stress worth while. The team provides primary experience for the least integrated boys in the commu-

---

[1] This paper was written in 1969.

nity (about eight or nine); and also provides reliable support for each other, without which such work cannot be achieved.

In this group of boys there is no mixture of integrated and unintegrated, so that the problems are simple (those of the unintegrated) rather than complex (those of the integrated). Boys who achieve some degree of integration in the Cottage either leave the community or go back into the main stream of community life. Now and then a boy asks to see me, usually when he is nearing recovery, but this is unusual. The boys in the Cottage know what I do, and discuss this with the team. When the Cottage project was launched, I gave the boys a fruit bowl, which stands in their little sitting room, and which I fill each week with fruit: there are no rules about this bowl of fruit, and they like the idea—they do not exploit or spoil the arrangement, and they explain the idea to newcomers. In this way I can assure them of my concern, without interrupting the treatment process in the Cottage by impingement.

The other houses in the community face rather different problems: mixtures of integrated and unintegrated boys, and more staff changes, perhaps, than in the Cottage. In these houses I have similar discussions with the teams: always open discussions of any theme which comes to the surface, but always linking themes to specific happenings. As I slowly became aware of this concept of incompatibility, which I have been thinking about, it seemed urgent to help the teams to *classify* their respective groups in terms of integration. We used the two factors which I have already mentioned—panic and disruption—to make a rough classification within each house: we have tried to consider integrated and unintegrated children as two groups needing different kinds of therapeutic management. I am by no means sure that this is possible, but at least the task is being attempted. Eventually I would hope that units could be smaller, and that boys could be established in groups planned on a basis of integration and consequent compatibility.

All houses have, for some time past, made use of a morning meeting for all the staff and boys of each unit every day. Great difficulties have been experienced in establishing communication in these groups, because of disruption and panic phenomena, with considerable acting out and immobilization (resulting from a breakdown in communication). By breaking down this large house meeting into small groups (four in each) on a basis of degree of integration, communication has been established. We hope to bring the small groups together (each with the grown-up leader) to form an integrated whole, when we are confident that there is sufficient functioning for this to be possible.[1]

I believe that if we can think in these terms, some of our major problems in residential work may be at least partially solved.

---

[1] Actually, we have never taken this step, because the small groups function so well.

4
Communicating stress in student supervision, 1969

This paper was read to a child care group, the members of which were all involved in student supervision. I feel that supervision of students in residential places is still sadly inadequate: a great deal remains to be thought out and properly structured in this area.

In chapter 1, 'Problems arising in the Communication of Stress', I discussed the communication of stress between deeply disturbed children and the adults who try to help them, in a residential treatment setting. I have been thinking a great deal about this subject, and want particularly to consider the problems attending the communication of stress by students and supervisors in relation to the supervision situation.

I recently read an interesting article by Janet Mattinson about the supervision of a student in a residential place by an outsider who knew both the student and the people who were running the place[1]. Reading this paper, I thought how fortunate are people who do their own supervision of students in a residential setting. Outside supervision is likely to cause splitting (between the people in the place and the supervisor) and an odd sort of collusion between the supervisor and the student, in regard to the people in the place.

Many students use their theoretical knowledge as a defence against having real experience. If they are being supervised from outside this becomes especially easy, because they can defend themselves against feelings of anxiety and inadequacy in the situation within the place, by intellectualizing what they are going through: so that they can in some way feel a conscious sense of superiority to the people in the place. It is difficult for an outside

[1] Janet Mattinson, 'Supervising a residential student'. *Case Conference*, April 1968, Vol. 14, No. 12.

supervisor to recognize this defence for what it is, a cover for anxiety. Where there is a supervisor inside the place (presumably one of the people who are in charge) such mechanisms become more obvious. For example, when a student in the therapeutic school where I work as a consultant says to the Head, 'Of course I am more likely to take an objective view of what is going on in the place than all of you who are so over-involved with the children', the Head is in a position to say, 'It must be awful for you, coming into a community like this, and feeling an outsider.'

Perhaps the real problem about the communication of stress is that people can very rarely report on what is happening inside them, except in retrospect. For example, a student who has, let us say, been in a panic state in regard to the management of a child's temper tantrum, may report on the tantrum as though he or she witnessed this quite calmly as an objective observer. Part of the trouble lies in the fact that the student, in common with many workers in the field of child care (and indeed, of all work with people) feels that to be professional is to be objective; and that the more detached, clearheaded and calm they appear to be, the more they will be accepted as a professional person. They are therefore liable to avoid talking much about how they really *feel* to their supervisors, in areas where they think that this may lead to critical judgements on their capacity as professional people.

It can on occasions be of value for the supervisor to be able to talk about his own experience of stress, in a way which helps the student to understand that realization and communication of stress make it manageable, and bring it within the total picture of what anyone experiences when working with other people. This may at first have the effect of shaking the confidence of the student in the supervisor; but gradually the fact that the supervisor is not alarmed or made to feel anxious or inadequate through the communication of stress may make it safer for the student also to talk about experience of stress. If the supervising person does not talk about his own difficulties in terms of experiencing stress, then the student is likely to be confirmed in his delusion that all professional people are invariably calm and detached in every situation.

It is interesting from this point to consider the *phenomenon* of stress. The extreme of this is panic, which has been described as 'unthinkable anxiety': it is the unthinkable quality which makes it impossible to communicate states of panic, except in very special circumstances. This is because unthinkable anxiety belongs originally to a pre-verbal era, when the baby who experienced something awful could not think about it but only feel, because he had no words with which to think.

There are, however, many degrees of stress which *can* be communicated; but it would seem vital that this should be as near the context as possible: communication will become more and more modified and rationalized in the passage of time. This makes me think that it is very important that students should be able to communicate to supervisors at all sorts of odd moments, rather than have an hour every week or a short time every evening, or any other such formal arrangement. The formal arrangement has its place, and an hour's discussion alone with the supervisor each week will be necessary and invaluable; the communication of stress is not so likely to turn up during such an hour as it is if the student knows that, in a moment when he is finding himself beyond his threshold of containable stress, he can come straight to the supervisor and talk about this, even if it is for only a very few minutes. The sheer *fact* of communication makes the stress tolerable, lowers the level of stress to where it can be contained; in other words, brings the stress within the particular threshold of the individual. The level of stress tolerance varies so enormously from person to person that this must be a highly individual matter. Flexibility in regard to communication can lead to a rising of this threshold in the individual, so that he will gradually find himself able to tolerate a higher degree of stress.

In recommending informal opportunities for the communication of stress I may be cutting across current ideas about the best way for supervisors to work, but I am deeply convinced about the importance of what I am saying, and you must consider my views for what they are worth, and discard them if you do not feel that they apply to your own work.

All of us inevitably do the sort of 'tidying up' I have described, in regard to our experiences; none of us can communicate really directly and honestly how we have felt and behaved in a particular context, if we have not satisfied our own standards in the situation. The longer we wait to discuss such adverse experiences which can be undermining to our morale the more likely are we to modify, distort, or alter what has happened to us. This is why I feel so strongly that immediate communication of stress is the only way in which such modification may be avoided, at least to a certain extent. This is especially true as the student gains confidence in the supervisor, because he is receiving sympathy and concern, rather than criticism and accusation, which is what he is expecting at first.

People have different aims when supervising students; obviously this must to some extent be so, because of the variation in the maturity and experience which the student brings to the placement. Some supervisors wish to impart as much knowledge, skills and techniques as may be practical in the particular setting. Other supervisors try to help the student to tolerate and gain some insight into the experiences which he communicates. Personally, I feel that knowledge, skills and techniques can only be used in a valuable way if they are based on experience, and realization of experience. Such experience is usually disturbing, and can raise the level of stress, and the student may avoid realization by one or the other of the defences which are at anyone's disposal; and, unless communication takes place, there may be an area of experience which the student may tend to avoid because it provokes anxiety.

Lisa, a student I was supervising, was experienced and clever. She brought me a happening for discussion.

Lucinda, a small patient of mine (of whom I have spoken before)[1], was building a little house for herself out of branches and leaves. Lisa found her trying to complete the house, and in some difficulty, particularly with the windows. Lisa offered to help, and in no time was established in the little house, making window-frames. Lisa described, and conveyed to me still, her intense pleasure; she said that this had been such fun, and then, rather hurriedly, that it was so nice to do something for Lucinda. Then she hesitated, and I asked her what had happened next. 'Well,' said Lisa unhappily, 'Lucinda went away and left me in the house –I suppose she got bored. She hasn't got much of an attention span–she drifts off out of situations, doesn't she?' I agreed that

---

[1] *Therapy in Child Care*, ch. 8.

this was so, but added that I felt Lisa was somehow worried about this happening, and asked if this was the case. Lisa at once admitted that she was indeed worried; she felt that she had made some mistake, although she had really helped Lucinda, who could not nerself have made window-frames. I suggested that here we might have found the core of the problem; perhaps Lucinda did not like someone else to achieve something beyond her own capacity.

We talked on about this happening, and various points emerged: the most important for Lisa was when she herself realized that what had seemed to her to be kindness and concern for Lucinda was really impingement of a rather awful kind, based on Lisa's wish for an opportunity to take over Lucinda's little house and play in it herself. This realization was reached gradually, working over every detail of the happening. Lisa had been under considerable stress, which was relieved through realization and communication. I was in a position to sympathize with Lucinda (who never did return to the house), and with Lisa, because it is awful to have to recognize ruthlessness and envy operating under cover.

Envy is likely to play quite a part in raising the stress level too high. This same student constantly expressed pity for me, and others: 'You have to work so hard!' or 'It must be awful for you, doing this all the time!' By pitying us she avoided admitting strong and disturbing envy; this eventually emerged in a recognizable form: 'How do you all work like this, without getting fed up and furious? Shall I ever achieve this sort of emotional economy?' This recognition of the envy underlying stress made Lisa's life much easier in the place.

Simple stress can be intolerable (for example, when one has to draw on exhausted emotional reserves when one is very tired); but complex stress, where unconscious envy, hate or guilt is also involved, may be expressed in ways which are destructive both to the worker under stress and to those with whom he comes in contact. Providing the stress can be communicated–the tip of the iceberg, as it were–then there is a good chance (even in complex stress) that the worker will dare to surface the deeper layers, to himself if not to others. In this connection I think it is important to respect the worker's privacy.[1] There *are* people who can contain and deal with a high level of stress within themselves: such people may be children or students. It can be disconcerting if we feel that in the circumstances the person *must* need to communicate stress, and even try to bring this about; when actually this is someone who has a high stress threshold, often because he can tolerate more than the usual amount of insight. We need to be available and accessible to students under stress; but we must leave it to them to choose whether or not to communicate their feelings, unless a point has been reached where the student is actually in reaction to stress, causing harm to others.

Another point which seems important is that the student and the supervisor will both need to be clear that provision of opportunity for communicating stress need not imply subsequent action. Very often, sympathetic and uncritical listening is all that is needed. The sufferer from stress cannot contain his feelings, and needs us to provide containment for the overflow. People often feel that something has got to be *done* at such a moment: I am certain that this is seldom the right time for decisions or actions.

The other danger is the natural wish of the supervisor to replace the often distorted picture presented by the student with the objective reality. This can lead to a logical argument, in the course of which the supervisor can show the student how far from objective reality is his reaction to a situation. However, the point has been missed: the reality which matters in such communication is the reality of the student's feelings—it is with these that the supervisor needs to be concerned, in the management of stress.

There is also the reality of the supervisor's feelings, which cannot be so easily communicated to the student; although, as I have suggested earlier in this paper, it is well worth while making it clear fairly early in the proceedings that we are not omnipotent or omniscient, and that we do not have magical powers which enable us to remain completely calm and undisturbed, in contrast to the rest of humanity. There are, however, problems connected with allowing students to know too much about our feelings.

[1] See ch. 1, p. 11.

I think one could say that one should only communicate enough to enable the student to make allowances for us, in particular circumstances. For example, if one is very worried for personal or professional reasons (or a mixture of the two) it is easy for this to ricochet off and hit the student or anyone else in the environment, without, of course, any intention on one's own part of allowing this to happen. I think it may be advisable in such circumstances to mention to the student, at a suitable moment, that one is in a worried, anxious state for all sorts of reasons; and ask them to bear this in mind if one is irritable or impatient. Otherwise the student, far from accusing one of being bad-tempered and difficult, will be sure that there is something the matter with his work, or that there is something in his personality of which we are showing our disapproval.

One sees this with parents and children: it is well worth while allowing one's children to know that one is worried or in a state about something, and to ask them to bear this in mind if one reacts in all sorts of ways which could be disturbing to them.

This is one of the difficulties of residential supervising, or indeed of residential work of any kind. One is not meeting someone in a session, in an office or consulting room or whatever, for just an hour, in which circumstances one can really be wholly concerned with one's client, although with the departure of the client all our worries will crowd once more into our minds. In residential work, we are coming into contact with other people all the time. The student may need to communicate stress to us just after we have heard that, for example, something has gone wrong with the management of the place, or that a child is in difficulties (perhaps in trouble with the police); and it is extremely difficult, if not impossible, to respond to the student's needs in such a context when we ourselves are under considerable stress. On such occasions I have found it valuable, when I have been deeply involved in residential work myself, to say, 'Of course you can talk to me for a few minutes about what is troubling you, but I may not be much use just now, because I'm worried about several things.' This does imply, of course, an acceptance of the fact that the supervisor is not so very different from the student: just as all residential child care workers have to be able to tolerate the realization that they are not so very different from the children for whom they are caring.

There are other areas where stress may be intolerable, and where communication to the student may present great difficulties. For example, it is possible for the supervisor to feel envy of the student. The student does not have the responsibilities which have to be accepted by the supervisor; the student comes for a short time – the period of the placement – and can then go away, while the supervisor remains to continue his work in the place; the student may have had opportunities which were denied to the supervisor; the very fact that the supervisor tends to be much older than the student can be another reason for experiencing stress complicated by envy. It is perhaps worth considering, whether or not it is desirable for such envy to be communicated to the student: possibly it is quite enough for the supervisor to realize this feeling, or to communicate the stress involved to a colleague; perhaps for this reason supervisors need supervisors! I wonder whether there are many people who can do this kind of work without the opportunity themselves of having some form of safety-valve through communication of stress.

Nobody would willingly get angry with a student or anybody else in a dependent role. Nevertheless, there must be moments when one does feel angry, perhaps due to some insensitivity on the student's part in relation to a disturbed child, or because the student has upset another member of staff or in some way undermined the confidence of a new worker who is just beginning to have some kind of morale in regard to his work in the place. Such a feeling of anger can be difficult to cope with in oneself: as with all types of stress, this feeling can be contained up to a certain level; all that is necessary as a rule is for one to know that one is feeling angry. But the moment many come when it rises above this threshold of toleration: one signal of this can be a physical aspect of anger. It is not for nothing that one talks of somebody going 'white with anger', or 'cold with rage': usually any high degree of stress is accompanied by some physical symptom, which may help one to recognize that one is at that moment beyond one's capacity to contain stress. At such a moment one needs to be extremely careful how one communicates with the student, because it would be terribly easy to be very destructive merely in order to relieve intolerable stress. Perhaps the best thing that one can do in these circumstances is to make a conscious effort to communicate one's concern for the person who has been damaged by the student, rather than one's anger with the student: after all, one's concern will also be a very deep and strong feeling: and after the first flash of anger inside oneself, one may be able to find a way of changing, as it were, one's channel of communication.

The student, on the other hand, may find it very difficult to get angry with us, or rather, the anger will certainly be there, but it will be hard for him to allow this feeling to become conscious, let alone communicable, because of his fears of retaliation. If he is able to get angry with you—in however intolerable a form this may appear, however rude, tiresome and bossy he may be—it is well to remember that the fact that he dares to get angry with you indicates that he trusts you; this is a considerable tribute to you as a person.

It is very easy for both supervisors and students alike to regard the communication of stress as a *symptom*. One can say that all symptoms are actually communications, but this is not to say that the reverse is true (not all communications are symptoms). It is wise to accept that we are all liable to stress; this is not a symptom, nor pathological. Communication can prevent uncontainable stress from turning into a symptom: for example, when one is angry, if one tries to hide the anger one may eventually have a bad headache; the headache *is* a sympton—one no longer feels the anger, which has been converted into the headache.

I feel that supervisors working within residential places with students have an opportunity to help to establish the communication of stress in the students' lives, which can eventually be of great use to both the students and the people with whom they will work later on.

5
Meeting children's emotional needs, 1969

This paper was read to a large Home Office group during a course at Nottingham University in 1969. It brings together a lot of learning experience in a way which led me to further realization. I remember my pleasure and surprise when I met so much sympathy and understanding in my audience (which included senior staff from approved schools). The discussion which followed was of value to me, and the next paper, 'Syndrome', presented during the same course also led to useful communication.

My point of view differs in many ways from that of other disciplines: for example, from that of a teacher. Much that I shall be suggesting may seem irrelevant in the present context of work in residential places: we are in a transitional phase between the publication of the new Act and its implementation. Clearly, there must be development and change—must there also be actual breaks in thought and practice? Are there some ideas or points of view which must be discarded, or can they be adapted to fit a new task?

There is a tendency, because of the close connection between physical and mental health, to think of psychotherapy of any kind as a treatment intended to lead to a cure. Accordingly (for example) the disappearance of specific symptoms in emotional disorder is taken as a sign of recovery; when in fact, the symptom may merely have shifted its ground. Sometimes a behaviour disorder may be replaced by physical symptoms, which will then be treated in the field of physical medicine: this is not a cure. I really wish to jettison the concept of 'cure' at once, and replace this by 'evolvement'. I believe that most people can evolve to some extent, however deeply disturbed they may be, and that in helping our clients to develop emotionally, we ourselves also evolve. There is for me no clear line of demarcation between psychotherapist and patient, teacher and pupil, child care worker and child: we are all *individual people*. Therapy, then, from my own particular viewpoint, involves a relationship between two or more people (individual or group therapy), used in a special and professional way, leading those concerned to further evolvement as unique human beings (Winnicott has pointed out that well people are unique, it is the ill ones who are stereotyped). This realization is essential, especially to those working with deprived and delinquent children. For example, therapeutic work will lead a delinquent to a special kind of depression: it is only too easy to mistake such a manifestation as evidence of deterioration rather than to welcome the onset of a depression as an indication of evolvement without which the delinquent's emotional life must remain static.

I have said that I do not see a clear boundary between workers and clients. Perhaps I should also make clear at this point the fact that I fail to see such a boundary between grownups and children. As I have said before, I regard the word 'adult' as a defence against the realization that we professional people are all *children who have grown up*. There are many parents who tell their children little or nothing about their own childhood: they need to deny the evolvement of the child into the grown-up, and cannot bear their children to think of them in such a way.

It will be realized that I am trying to set up a clear field of communication in which to work. I want my own personal outlook to be understood: it seems important that I should make my position clear. So, I am saying that grown-ups trying to help disturbed children to evolve will *themselves* evolve, provided they can allow relationships to come into existence between grown-ups and children, of which therapeutic use can be made. Just as I am not prepared to think of grown-ups as being other than children grown up, so I am also unwilling to ignore the fact that a sixteen-year-old can have the same needs as the six-months-old, although these needs may be communicated in a distorted, broken down way (we call this 'acting out'). If these needs are not met at six months, or six years or sixteen years or twenty-six years, they will not *change*. The approved schools are having to compensate for the failure of the residential nurseries. One could say of the 'outside' child whom we meet in the approved school, that the shell is made up of defences (to hide the real self) and of broken down communication, taking the form of deviant behaviour. We have to try to understand the nature of the defences, and the communication implicit in the behaviour.

I am advocating a therapy based on *needs* rather than *symptoms*, bearing in mind that many of our clients have been traumatized in one way or another: we are often trying to treat emotionally damaged people who need corrective experience ('corrective' in this sense has no punitive implications). Just what experience may be needed depends on the stage of integration reached by each individual: we need to classify children according to needs based on degree of integration reached. Such classification can be carried out within any kind of residential unit by the people working in the place. If the treatment of the kind I am considering is to become available to the thousands in need of help, then residential units must shoulder the responsibility of providing therapy themselves, rather than looking to outside agencies. This applies equally to residential nurseries and to community homes. Anybody doing residential work with children and young people must learn to make use of therapeutic skills. We have an enormous emotional refugee problem on our hands: thousands of emotionally starved children who are all, in the deepest sense of the word, displaced people. There is nobody beyond us to whom we can hand over this responsibility. Furthermore, a therapy of provision leading to evolvement is not available in a child guidance clinic: such treatment can only be appropriately given in a residential setting, relating as it does to the entire life of the child in need.

It is important that this work should be seen as active, skilled and economic. I am not talking about a permissive environment with minimal controls and structure. There will certainly be no place for corporal punishment or other archaic punitive practices in the new community homes, but it is no use forbidding one kind of management unless it be replaced by another—certainly nothing can evolve in a vacuum. I am, of course, well aware that therapeutic work, such as I have described is being carried out already and I want this to become more conscious and more communicated.

I have spoken of the necessity for classification within a residential unit, based on need and on stage of integration. I must clarify my use of the term 'integration', which is based on Winnicott's concept of integration *as an individual*. I am sure that many of you are accustomed to thinking of integrated or unintegrated children; but, so far, it does not seem usual for residential staff to classify the children in a unit on this basis. When I speak of integration, I am thinking on the lines which Winnicott has postulated.

The populations of residential nurseries, children's homes, and schools for the maladjusted and (up to the present) approved schools, are made up in nearly all cases of a mixture of integrated and unintegrated children. It is essential that the needs of all deprived children should be met: and it must be clearly understood that the nature of these needs depends on degree of integration. So far, it is usual for the behaviour of unintegrated children to be recognized as 'different' from that of others, and to attach labels to them such as behaviour disorders, character disorders, psychopathic personalities, and so on. These labels—technical or otherwise—emphasize the difference between these children and others, while totally failing to suggest that (although they cannot benefit from what is available in the way of management) they are in need of special treatment: this need is so much less easy to recognize, for many reasons, in unintegrated children than in integrated, functioning children, especially because of the breakdown of communication into acting out.

The therapist working with integrated children depends on transference phenomena and on verbal interpretation within the strict limits of the therapeutic hour. The therapist working with unintegrated children must depend on personal involvement, on symbolic actions (adaptations) and on re-establishing communication in place of acting out.

I have worked in two units as a consultant; one catering for five- to twelve-year-olds and specializing in the treatment of severely emotionally deprived unintegrated children who are selected on this basis, and the other an approved school which is still in the difficult phase of change from approved school to therapeutic community. In the first unit (the Mulberry Bush), the only integrated children are those who have evolved to a point at which they are nearly ready to leave the school. In the second (the Cotswold Community) there is at all times a mixture of barely integrated and unintegrated adolescents. It has been possible to classify the approved school children by assessment of integration in the four house groups. This kind of assessment is not usually available in referral reports, but I have found that residential staff are quite able to carry out this sort of in-living diagnosis themselves, in consultation with me. We have used two factors only, in assessing degree of integration: these have been panic and disruption. Where both these factors are present we assume unintegration. Both phenomena are easy to recognize, once their nature is understood. Panic is often described as temper tantrum: disruption as antisocial behaviour. *Panic*, rarely mentioned in psychiatric reports, is the hallmark of unintegration, and represents traumatic–unthinkable–experience at an early age. It produces claustrophobia and agoraphobia, states of disorientation and a total loss of any sense of identity: the victim falls to pieces in a state beyond terror. He may be totally immobilized; or, more frequently, he may hit out, scream, destroy things or attack other people. *Disruption*, described by Erikson as play disruption, can be seen in action very easily. The child comes into a situation where others are functioning, either in work or play, and at once compulsively breaks into the group and breaks up the activity. Panic and disruption are familiar to any experienced worker, but may not have been seen as signals of distress.

It is easier to pick out children who are not integrated, rather than to describe those who are whole, functioning people. My own experience leads me to suppose that in a group of twelve children in residential care–let us say in a children's home–probably two or three will be unintegrated. These children will have an obvious and harmful influence on the lives of the integrated members of the group; while the integrated, functioning children will have very little counter-influence on those who are unintegrated. The mixture of integrated and unintegrated seems to be disastrous for both groups, unless we can find ways of meeting very different needs in the same environment (see chapter 3). I believe this to be possible: whether economic is questionable. On the whole, I feel that there is something to be said for classification to take place as early as possible within the unit, so that living groups can be constituted from similar ingredients, rather than from an explosive mixture of elements.

Within the Cotswold Community there is now a cottage which contains the least integrated group in the community. I think, from what I have seen so far that the cottage group remains therapeutically viable, despite inevitable changes of staff and inmates. On the other hand, each of the eight or nine children in the cottage would cause havoc in other groups: from time to time an unintegrated boy arrives into the community who cannot be placed in the cottage, and one can then see only too clearly how disruptive his presence can be in another group, and how easily he can become either a delinquent hero or a scapegoat. In the same way, any one of the thirty younger children in the Mulberry Bush School would be 'the impossible one' in any normal class, but each becomes manageable in an environment which meets his needs.

I have suggested that a classification of needs can be made, based on two factors–the presence of panic and disruption. Obviously this is a rough-and-ready way to work, and there will always be some borderline cases where it will be difficult to decide the degree of integration. The later the stage of evolvement reached, the less obvious will be the lack of integration. However, nothing can be absolute, and assessment must always be tentative and experimental.

What follows is a scheme or chart, which lists assumptions, aims and techniques, in regard to integrated and unintegrated people of any age, from the standpoint of a psychotherapist. One would say that there must always, in *any* case, be a contract between therapist and patient; a process, whatever needs to to happen between them–evolvement of the patient *and* the therapist.

INTEGRATED	UNINTEGRATED
1. *Assumptions*	
good enough start	not good enough start
identity	projective identification
possibility of transference	no transference, involvement
capacity for guilt	no capacity for guilt
defences, e.g. repression	primitive defences, splitting
boundary between conscious and unconscious	no barrier between conscious and unconscious
symbolization	no symbolization
capacity to contain experiences	

2. *Aims*

sorting out the past	filling gaps in experience
to resolve conflict through transference	to achieve integration as a person
break down crippling defences	through adaptation to reach
enable patient to make full use of potential	regression, containment, with build-up of defences to reach personal guilt, repression, and so on.

3. *Techniques*

use of transference interpretation	involvement with realization
	symbolic communication
	adaptation
surfacing of repressed material	

4. *Therapeutic management*

not needed	needed in some or all areas

Very special and long training, including personal analysis, is required to treat integrated patients: in residential work, much that we can achieve for such children depends on our ability to be suitable people with whom children can identify.

We assume that integrated children can identify, having reached secondary experience; but that in the past parental figures have been in some way inadequate: we have to compensate for such inadequacies. The parents will hate and envy us because we are able to help their children in a way which they cannot achieve. We cannot assume that unintegrated children can identify, because they have not reached secondary experience. Here we have to supply missing primary experience, which their deprived parents (or staff in institutions) have been unable to supply. We can expect these parents also to hate us, but they will *envy their children* rather than ourselves, because such parents will know that they themselves have these primary needs (see chapter 2).

Therapeutic work with integrated children in residential treatment is more complex, but less exacting, than work with unintegrated children. Once integrated, children can transfer the deep confused feelings they have for their parents to us, giving us an opportunity to understand these feelings, and to help them to do so, thereby freeing them to identify with us in a new way. We have to ask ourselves whether we as people can offer them a better chance to evolve in relation to us and our way of life. It is not painful to reach understanding of their difficulties, but it can be very painful to be understood by them—sometimes better than we understand ourselves.

Unintegrated children present quite other problems. We have to provide experience which is actually missing from their lives. They will, in time, accept us with a devastating degree of trust and dependence. There will be no transference in the ordinary sense—they cannot transfer what they have not got. They will be involved with us and we with them in a very simple and primitive way: our reliability will become our most valuable therapeutic tool.

Here, then, are the two main groups to be found in all residential work. How much therapy can be carried out in any residential unit by the people in the place? What is the nature of such therapy? How can we actually help children to evolve?

Our first task is to produce a suitable emotional climate in the place, for therapy to be possible. We need to remember that a therapist, basically, is not a person *doing*, but a person *being*: for example, people can stop actually punishing but remain punitive. The right words are no use if they are only a cover for the wrong feelings. Since child care workers cannot have a personal analysis and a distinct training as therapists, we need to evolve a mainly 'do-it-yourself' approach, which may help them to gain insight and free them to become professionally involved with children in this special way.

People tend to think of therapeutic work as being carried out in a clinic or consulting room in the course of formal sessions, over a considerable period of time. Therapy in child care is concerned with the content of the total life situation in the place, including waking and sleeping, eating and drinking, working and playing and so on.

To produce the essential emotional climate, if it is not already present, we need to 'clear the decks'. We can most easily make a start in the field of communication, which can become a desert in residential work. There is a tendency to use stereotyped phrases in talking to children, or about them. Workers hide behind these phrases, and the children do likewise: as a result, real feelings are not communicated unless they burst through under stress in the brokendown form which we call 'acting out' (punishment is often acting out). There are various ways of establishing real communication in residential work. You will all be familiar with the writings of David Wills:[1] the concepts of self-government, democratic participation and shared responsibility all involve open and free communication between grown-ups and children; in the course of which, feelings and ideas can be expressed, and respected and used by all. I feel that this sort of approach is ideal for integrated children who have had a good enough start in emotional life, and who are able therefore to experience, realize and conceptualize adequately, in a way which unintegrated children cannot do. Children are encouraged by such work to accept responsibility for being themselves.

At the same time, we must provide them with objects for identification—ourselves. This means in practice a great deal of self-awareness. The worker functioning as a therapist must do so as himself, but with concern, so that he speaks and acts in a responsible and sensitive way in the place. The avoidance of direct and real communication between workers and children aims at preventing the formation of deep personal relationships —which are essential for therapeutic purposes. Therefore, once such communication is established, we can expect these relationships to come spontaneously into existence. When children are integrated, they will transfer to us their conflicts in regard to their parents, and we are then in a position to understand something of their difficulties; and by communicating our understanding, to help them to evolve from long static positions in regard to others.

Institutionalization is a defence against emotional processes: de-institutionalize, and we produce a climate in which these processes can develop *through which people can evolve*. Lack of real

[1] See David Wills, *Throw Away Thy Rod*, Gollancz 1960

communication has a depersonalizing effect, and the establishment–or re-establishment–of communication is an essential
first measure to make therapeutic work possible.

It is a much easier task to establish communication with integrated children than with unintegrated ones. The latter group
must be considered carefully because this is the source of most
problems in any residential work. I have already mentioned the
tendency of unintegrated children to panic and to disrupt the
functioning of others. I have found that small groups of four
children and one grown-up, meeting each morning for about
half an hour, can eventually reach intercommunication. Such
a group can be mixed in degree of integration (a ratio of one
unintegrated to three integrated), but ideally *not* mixed, so that
the functioning of the integrated does not threaten the unintegrated. The beginning of such work will probably be extremely
discouraging, but communication will come with patience and
empathy.

In order to understand the therapeutic value of invariable
response to all communication from children of any age, it is
important to grasp the concept of 'the spontaneous gesture'
(Winnicott). The baby smiles at the mother and reaches out to
her: the mother's response is an essential to the baby's emotional
wellbeing. If the mother does not or cannot (because of her own
defences) respond to the spontaneous gesture, then the baby
is reaching out as though for ever into infinity. Eventually in
such a case the baby ceases to attempt those gestures, having
reached despair. Our response to what a deprived child tries to
communicate may re-establish his belief in the possibility of response to his reaching out. Recently a child aged ten called Timothy
drew for me a picture of himself in his cot as a baby: the picture
showed him lying flat in the cot with one hand showing between
the bars. He said, 'That's me trying to reach my mum–it's a bit
like a cage, the cot, isn't it?' I replied that this was so, but that
perhaps the bars of this cage also kept his mother away from him
–were also the bars of *her* cage: in other words, her defences,
protecting him from her violence, but also isolating him.

We have to be careful that children find *us* when they reach
out, and that they do not again find defences instead of people.
A boy at the Cotswold Community said to me: 'It's different

here from the other place.' I asked what was the greatest difference, to which he answered: 'People really listen to you—they don't just hear you—they *listen*—nobody has ever listened to me like that before.'

Sometimes people are afraid of what children will say, of the dreadful unanswerable questions they may ask: this is a valid fear, but it is also valid to say that just listening is therapy. At first much that our clients will say will be paranoid accusations and complaints against all who are in authority of any kind, complaints without logical reasoning. We can listen to such complaints, accepting the reality of the feelings expressed and leaving the objective reality alone for the present. Gradually the child will start to communicate his dread and his helplessness.

We are, I assume, considering the whole range of residential displacement, residential nurseries, children's homes, schools for maladjusted children, and approved schools. In all these institutions I suspect that there is a larger proportion of unintegrated children than is realized—this is not a policy, but a relatively unconsidered fact.

Let us now take a look at the needs of these unintegrated children. With integrated neurotic children, we can assume the presence of an identity, a functioning ego, a capacity for concern (personal guilt), and anxiety (repressed guilt). None of these assumptions hold good when we come to consider those who have not achieved the establishment of identity. We are now considering the terribly deprived ones—those whose needs have not been met during the first year of life. I have elsewhere described[1] the syndromes which develop in terms of the nature of the traumatic interruption of emotional development and the point at which this has taken place. Here I must quote my descriptions of these syndromes of deprivation.

The most primitive of these categories, that is to say the least integrated, is made up of those whom I have described elsewhere as the 'frozen' children; who have suffered interruption of primary experience at the point where they and their mothers

[1] *Therapy in Child Care,* ch. 9, 'The provision of primary experience in a therapeutic school'.

[1] *Ibid.,* p. 99.

would be commencing the separating out process, having been as it were broken off rather than separated out from their mothers. They have survived by perpetuating a pseudosymbiotic state; without boundaries to personality, merged with their environment, and unable to make any real object relationships or to feel the need for them.

Such a child must be provided with the actual emotional experiences of progression to separating out; thereby establishing identity, accepting boundaries, and finally reaching a state of dependence on the therapist. This kind of child cannot symbolize what he has never experienced or realized. (A 'frozen' child, on referral, will steal food from the larder because he wants food at that moment and for no other reason. The same child in the course of recovery may steal again from the larder, because his therapist is absent; this stealing will now be symbolic.)

The next category consists of those who have achieved the first steps towards integration; so that one could describe them as made up of ego-islets which have never fused into a continent—a total person. For this reason we call them 'archipelago' children. These children give the impression of being quite mad whenever they are not being quite sane. They are either wildly aggressive, destructive, and out of touch in states of panic-rage or terror; or they are gentle, dependent, and concerned. They present a bewildering picture till one comes to know them and to understand the meaning of their behaviour. They too need to progress through the process of integration. However, these stormy children are not so difficult to help as 'frozen' children, because the presence of ego-islets amid the chaos of unassimilated experience makes life more difficult for them. They are, from time to time, very unhappy and aware that they need help. The fact that some primary experiences have been contained and realized results in their having a limited capacity for symbolization, which facilitates communication of a symbolic kind which is not available to 'frozen' ones. Where 'frozen' and 'archipelago' children are concerned, treatment must involve the breakdown of pathological defences, containment of the total child, and the achievement of dependence on the therapist as a separate person. These two groups, in which integration has not been sufficient to establish a position from which to regress, are very different from those in the next category.

Classifying the 'false-self' organizations, Winnicott writes: 'At one extreme: the false-self sets up as real and it is this that observers tend to think is the real person. In living relationships, work relationships, and friendships, however, the false-self begins to fail. In situations in which what is expected is a whole person the false-self has some essential lacking. At this extreme the true-self is hidden.' Having described other types of false-selves advancing towards health, he continues: 'Still further towards health: the false-self is built on identifications (as for example that of the patient mentioned whose childhood environment and whose actual nannie gave much colour to the false-self organization).'

The latter organization he has described as the 'caretaker-self'. This elaborate defence takes various forms, and is often difficult to recognize, especially because the 'little self' part of the child is carefully concealed by the caretaker (for example, there may be a delinquent 'caretaker' which steals without conflict, on behalf of the 'little-self').

Therapeutic work with these deeply deprived children involves one in making adaptations to their needs, much as the 'ordinary devoted mother' (Winnicott) makes adaptations to the needs of her babies. It is important to realize at once that there is nothing impossible about this task, which is being carried out constantly in therapeutic institutions. The easiest approach is to introduce certain adaptations oneself, which become 'part of life'. As I have said before, all children should have hotwater bottles, a special drink, and the chance to communicate when they are in bed, before they go to sleep. Such provision will soon become highly individual. A child will choose a bottle of this colour, will write his name on it, will need it filled so full and so hot, and for the bottle to be placed in his bed, or given to him, or whatever. You can see how depersonalization can be tackled by such means. Provision like this can be made either based on an individual relationship established between child and grown-up, or between the child and the house team. In any event there must be constant communication between members of the treatment team, so that everybody becomes aware of the individual needs of each child. While it is always difficult to embark on provision, the rewards are so instant that the work becomes easier as staff gain confidence.

Food is an area of provision which is all too often utterly institutionalized. Delinquent excitement is frequently a displacement from frustrated infantile greed. Food available when needed can often help to bring this excitement back into the oral zone where it belongs. There must be plenty of milk and snacks available on request (as Derek Miller found):[1] but the food, in my view, should always *be given by somebody*, rather than be collected by the child from the larder.

Society tends to be punitive in regard to food in institutions: not enough money is assigned to food in the budget; cooking is impersonal, in bulk, and frequently unappetising. Ideally each group should be eating in the unit or cottage, rather than with the whole population in one large dining hall. It is interesting to note that meals eaten in small groups take much longer than those *en masse*, because the children talk and enjoy themselves personally over a meal in their own group, whereas they eat their food and go as soon as possible when eating in a dining hall.

Children in rigid institutions are constantly exposed to further frustration and deprivation, which lead, of course, to subcultures and depravity–for which they are punished, thus creating a vicious circle.

Many people in child care would spontaneously work in the way I have described: they often only need permission, encouragement and support to become therapists. Very often in a rigid institution such workers may be criticized, discouraged and undermined: this is true in every field–in hospitals, schools, and children's homes. Leadership roles in a therapeutic community must be distinct and reliable. The 'director' (or whatever he may be termed), the head of group living, the head of each unit, or the housemother, must be linked by principles and free communication on a basis of mutual support. Women need to be able to work professionally and in role, not confining their activities to mending and housework. A group of men and women working together as therapists, helping each other to understand the problems of the children in their care, can achieve a high standard of therapeutic skill. They will need to read, and to talk over and apply what they read to their experience, in order to learn how to add therapeutic attitudes to their various skills and to accept roles within their specific functions as teachers, craftsmen or houseparents.

I was involved in a very interesting and valuable experience

---

[1] See Derek Miller, *Growth to Freedom*, Tavistock 1964, pp. 109 and 178.

which took place between a carpentry instructor and a deprived delinquent boy. Tommy had become interested in chess and the history of the game. He could play very well, and he decided that he wished to make his own chess set. He was interested in an eighteenth century chess set which I had been given, and I brought a piece to show him. He was fascinated by the survival of the set, and wondered about the craftsmen who had carved the pieces with such skill, so long ago. He suggested that if he now made a chess set, this might also survive into some future century, and in any case he could hand the set down to his son. This was the first time I had heard Tommy talking about any distant future or past (like most delinquents, he lived in the present exclusively). I explained about Tommy's wish to the carpentry instructor, who gave him the considerable amount of help and support that he needed to carve the queen, which he brought to show me on my next visit. Subsequently he carved the king, and then a remarkably fat pawn (he is a solid little person himself). Tommy was delighted by his achievement, and we all eagerly awaited further developments.... There were none. Tommy was satisfied by what to him was a complete experience. He had symbolized a family – a father, a mother and one child, which was what he would have wished his family to be. A chess set became irrelevant in terms of his symbolization. Nobody urged him to continue a task which, however incomplete for us, was finished for him: he values his three pieces highly, and so do we all. Here is an example of therapeutic work action within the normal structure of a residential place.

I have written a paper on the subject of therapeutic play in residential work:[1] I find it difficult to condense such a large subject into any sort of summary. I have suggested that—in common with other therapeutic measures—therapeutic play depends on the provision of a suitable emotional climate. Everyone is ready to teach children how to play games: therapeutic play comes from inside the children themselves, many of whom have never played in this symbolic way. There is, however, no need to interpret this sort of play—to tease out the meaning of the children's use of play material: interpretation of play belongs to play therapy, whereas opportunities for therapeutic play can be provided by

[1] See 'Play as therapy in child care' *Therapy in Child Care,* ch. 11

workers in residential places of all kinds, and for children of all ages.

You will realize from what I have said that here again, the play groups need to be classified into integrated and unintegrated, with never more than eight children in a group, with one therapist-worker.

There will always be occasional children who need more intensive treatment—psychotherapy or even hospitalization. Such decisions can only be reached on the advice of a consultant psychiatrist. It would seem that there will be intensive care units for very ill children who need to be insulated and contained for treatment to be possible. Most children, however, could be treated within the proposed framework of a community home, where (presumably) a child guidance team will be available to the whole community. I would hope that some of the work of such a team would be available for use in the further training of staff, through lectures, films and discussion groups.

At first any consultant will be felt as a threat to the people in the place; then, probably, in the next phase as some sort of magical messiah 'who knows all the answers'. Eventually, however, there is a good chance that the consultant will be reasonably in role, working in a structured and carefully planned way, known to all and used economically and to further primary tasks (i.e. not regarded as a resource for the grown ups, to the exclusion of the children).

As a consultant psychotherapist I work in the two units already mentioned on much these lines. Most of my work takes the form of group discussions: at the Mulberry Bush I also meet the child care staff as a group, and I have an individual session with each member of the team every week. I see children 'on demand' for short or long sessions, and I meet the headmaster weekly. All these meetings are based on whatever people wish to discuss with me, with the exception of one weekly meeting with the whole team (about fifteen people), when we consider a context profile which has been built up by everyone, including myself. This kind of reporting in depth seems to have special values in residential work. In order to make a context profile, the team choose a child for special consideration, and then report on all their experiences (not observations) with this child in the course of a week. At the end of a week, during which I have a session with the child, we meet to pool experiences, and discuss the implications in terms of the child's own needs, and how these can be met at this point. This is an oversimplified description: 'Context profiles' is a paper in *Therapy in child care.*

SUMMARY

I must apoligize for the fact that I have as it were painted a picture, instead of producing a blue-print for therapy in residential work. I hope, however, that I have succeeded in showing you, what many of you must already know, that therapy belongs within the context of everyday life in a place. There can be no therapeutic work without the foundation of relationships between grown-ups and children: you cannot do therapy in an emotional vacuum, however precise the dosage.

There must be *communication*–real, uncensored communication, which means that grown-ups at all levels have to listen in a very special way to anything which children say, however apparently rude or irrelevant. There must also be this real communication between the grown-ups themselves, who can then pool their resources. There will be adaptation to individual needs in groups– provision of primary and transitional experience among un-integrated children, and opportunites and support for functioning among integrated children. For this to be possible there must be classification according to integration, and assessment and re-assessment of stage of integration reached. There is a need for consultation to be available to grown-ups and children, individually and in groups.

But above all, therapy needs to be seen as a recognition of needs –deep, urgent needs–which must be met with concern.

6
Syndrome, 1970

I have already mentioned (p. 50) that this paper was read during a Home Office course at Nottingham University in 1969. My intention is to write other 'syndromes' describing all the syndromes of deprivation (described in 'The Provision of primary experience', 'Therapy in Child Care, ch.9).

I am going to try in this paper to describe a syndrome of deprivation—what Winnicott calls 'caretaker self'. I described this syndrome briefly in Chapter 5.

I want to convey to you the *feeling* of this syndrome; how it appears in a baby in a residential nursery, in a child in a children's home, a school for maladjusted children, and finally in an approved school. All my descriptions will be real, in that they will be based on actual clinical material about severely emotionally deprived children at different ages. Ideally, I should be giving the whole history of one such child, but I have never had the opportunity of tracing such an individual from babyhood to adolescence. What I have actually done, therefore, is to build the early history on case material and clinical descriptions of deprivations in early childhood. Subsequently, I shall be able to quote from personal experience with actual 'caretaker-selves' at later stages in residential places and from discussion with people working with them.

What is so striking about any syndrome of deprivation is the lack of change in the child (or indeed, adolescent or grown-up). Their defences remain as established in babyhood, until their needs are met—when at last they can begin to grow emotionally.

My first piece of clinical material will describe the formation of the caretaker-self syndrome during the first year of the life of a baby whom I shall call James. James was an illegitimate child: his mother was a girl of sixteen, herself deprived and delinquent. We know nothing about his father, and practically nothing concerning his mother, who handed James over for adoption and disappeared for ever from his life, when he was about three weeks old. His actual birth was prolonged and traumatic, and he was a delicate baby. He was adopted by a couple, Mr and Mrs B, who were devoted to him. Mrs B was capable of the deep maternal preoccupation without which he probably would not have survived: because of the following months in Mrs B's care, James gained enough primary experience to build an ego—a self, fragile and delicate like a young plant, but established through her love and reliability.

When James was about nine months old, Mrs B died as the result of a sudden illness. Mr B was inconsolable. His own parents and those of Mrs B were very involved with the baby; they introduced into the house a nurse-housekeeper, to take charge of James under their guidance, and to run the house for Mr B. This housekeeper, Mrs Smith, was a cold, efficient person. She took every care of James from a physical point of view, but was rigid and punitive in her management of him, so that he was deprived of maternal love, and was looked after in an institutionalized way. Mr B was so sunk in mourning for his wife that he put all his energy into his business. When at home, however, he was kind and concerned about James—but too exhausted and unhappy to realize how emotionally ill James was becoming. The grandparents on both sides approved of Mrs Smith's care of James: but from the first they over-indulged and stimulated him in a way which had nothing to do with the baby's needs—but everything to do with their own. There was rivalry between both pairs of grandparents, and a sort of possessiveness in regard to James, but more as a thing than a person.

As I have said, James had been able to establish a fragile ego from the good experience given to him by his adoptive mother. Now he was no longer picked up and held when he cried; and he was fed on a rigid schedule, not when he was hungry. At first he was inconsolable: he cried incessantly, refused food, had constant digestive upsets, and slept very badly. It was noticed that he put his thumbs under his armpits, apparently trying to raise himself: I think that at this point (aged ten months) he was trying to *be* the mother who used to lift him up in her arms. Because he now often had to wait too long for his feeds, he would become desperately excited and greedy, but eventually lose the excitement and greed; so that by the time Mrs Smith brought his feed, he was not excited any more, though he accepted the feed. Presently the excitement became split off from food and was felt in other contexts (eventually this orgiastic excitement went into the field of delinquency).

James became apparently completely accepting of the rigid regime imposed by Mrs Smith. He was habit trained early, was clean and 'good', rarely cried, but continued to sleep very little. He responded to stimulation with apparent delight, but he did nothing spontaneous. He *returned* smiles, but he did not initiate any communication. Somehow he managed to maintain a sort of inner reality. He himself became the mother who looked after her baby–his real self. The 'mother' part of him, however, became modelled on the pattern of Mrs Smith. One could say that the harsh introjected super-ego of Mrs Smith took over the care of the fragile ego-id which was James himself. He became extremely reserved, inhibited and secret, hiding his real self in order to insure his survival. He became in effect *two* people: James the stern nurse guarding his charge, and James the instinctual, frantic and excited baby – hidden for the most part, but always present within him.

From time to time the defence–the caretaker–broke down, and James would become very ill, running high temperatures: these illnesses puzzled the family doctor. One day it would be the instinctual, excited little self which would break away into delinquency, but this was years later. We leave James at eighteen months.

Peter was the third and youngest child of a fairly united marriage. His elder brother and sister were aged eight and nine when he was born, so that in a way he was rather like an only child. He was unplanned, but not unwanted, nevertheless his arrival on the scene presented problems. Both his parents were working, and his mother, Mrs M, had become used to the professional life to which she had returned when the older children started school. Mrs M, like Mrs B, was capable of maternal preoccupation with her babies. This tie proved stronger than her wish to return to work for the first few months of Peter's life (his birth was normal). For various reasons Mrs M's unmarried sister lived with the family at this time, and once Peter was weaned, Mrs M arranged with

her sister–Miss C–that she should take over the care of Peter.
who had, up to this point, been a normal and happy baby. Mr M
was glad that this was possible, because Mrs M's earnings made a
considerable difference to the family income. Mrs M was only
devoted to her babies for the first months of their lives. This plan
need not have been disastrous had the sister, Miss C, been a
maternal person who could have to some extent represented his
mother, providing transitional experience which could have
prevented deprivation. As it was, the long periods which Peter
spent in the care of Miss C became for the most part gaps in emotional experience–gaps, because they were unthinkable. These
histories of severe deprivation all stem from a pre-verbal period,
so that only pre-verbal communication is available: babies cannot
think about their troubles, only *feel* them.

Peter spent long periods sitting silent and 'well behaved' in
his cot or pram: his world, seen in this way, remained two-di-
mensional. He had no opportunities to discover the depth of his
environment through tactile experience. This perceptual problem
was later to result in disorientation and severe panic states (these
were really states of helpless rage). I want you to imagine Peter,
at the age of eighteen months and about two feet high, standing
at the top of a staircase. The stairs from his viewpoint would
appear as a smooth precipice. Normally he would have discovered
the steps by sitting with his mother and bumping gently down
them. Peter was deprived of such experience, so that he became
terrified of stairs. Perhaps his aunt, Miss C, *explained* to him about
the nature of a staircase, but this was no use to him at all. This is
the mistake that so many people make–to suppose that conceptualization can precede experience. This is only one example of
failure in adaptation.

Miss C left Peter's home when he was just two years old. The
damage was already done; Peter was a conforming, grave little
boy, always quiet, polite and obedient. He ate little, slept badly
and was beginning to have severe attacks of panic, which were
seen as temper tantrums. He also had physical breakdowns into
respiratory illness. His mother felt that he was now her sister's
child: because of lifelong problems between them, she unconsciously rejected Peter, who now seemed so like her sister, Miss C.

Peter's mother suddenly became ill and was hospitalized. The older children went to stay with their grandmother in the country. Peter, on the advice of the family doctor, was placed in a small residential nursery near his home. Those of you who have seen the latest Robertson film 'John' will have some idea of the dangers implicit in such a placement. John, however, was a normal integrated little boy when he entered the nursery: Peter was already so damaged that this placement only strengthened the pathological defence. The workers in the nursery found him cooperative and quiet. Nobody thought of him as a seriously ill little boy: nobody saw his so *very* good and prim behaviour as evidence of deep deprivation. They noticed that he preferred to stay in one place, that he did not eat much, and was not physically strong. One worker described him as 'old-fashioned'. Most of the other small children in the nursery had been institutionalized for some time. They rushed about, were excited and aggressive, communicated in an institutionalized way, and tended to attack Peter. The workers were unfailingly kind, and physical standards were excellent, but they had no insight into the problems of deprivation; and the terrible shift system (*still* in existence) made any continuity of care by one person impossible.

By the end of the months which Peter had spent in the nursery— although he was visited by his father—he was doomed. He was not to find the primary experience he needed until he was fifteen years old. Until then, nobody except Peter himself knew of the existence of his real self. He led a narrow, restricted life, interrupted by illness and panic states, until his breakdown in adolescence.

Very little could be established about Richard's early life because his mother was terribly vague and unreliable. His father had left when Richard was a baby: he was taken into care when he was about two years old and was placed in a foster home. Mrs V, his foster mother, loved him deeply, and from various bits of evidence it seems that he must have had a much needed regression to a baby— hood state in this home. By this, I mean the organized regression of which Winnicott writes; in which the patient returns to that point at which maternal adaptation failed, and receives in actual or symbolic form the kind of care which is needed by babies, thereby filling the gaps in emotional experience which are always to be found in cases of emotional deprivation. Five years later, Richard could convey to me the warmth and security which he felt during this period with Mrs V.

This was not to last. Mrs V and her husband wished to adopt Richard–but at this point Richard's mother suddenly demanded that he should be returned to her. Unimaginably, Richard was dragged away from a despairing Mrs V. He said to me later: 'They must have known–we both cried and cried.' The Vs left the district. Richard meanwhile struggled miserably with his own family. He could not talk about Mrs V at home: he tried not to lose all that she meant to him, whilst keeping his love–and his despair– secret. He developed the symptom of soiling, which was in fact symbolic communication of his inability to keep the secret of his hidden need for Mrs V. His mother rejected him and was so punitive towards him that he was again taken into care (at her request), and established in a children's home at the age of five years.

Here he continued to soil, and to keep his real self (the baby who had had a start with Mrs V) hidden from everybody. Apart from the soiling symptom, Richard was not a difficult child to manage, although the staff in the home found him cold and reserved.

In this case we can see the formation of the caretaker–self syndrome at a much later stage of development. One can assume that Richard had a very bad start with massive deprivation during the first year. By the time he reached Mrs V, he was probably as institutionalized, cold and violent as the toddlers in the film of 'John'.[1] He would probably have emerged as a 'frozen' delinquent, but Mrs V's provision brought about a change in direction: Richard had a therapeutic breakdown in her care which strengthened his embryonic ego. The traumatic separation from her resulted in the caretaker (the Richard who was rigid, cold and reserved) and the 'secret' little self, built from the experience with Mrs V, but of necessity hidden from his jealous and rejecting mother, and subsequently from everyone. Much later, when I met him in treatment in a therapeutic school, I asked, 'But Richard, why have you never talked about this before to anyone?' He replied: 'There was never anyone to talk *to*–nobody who would

[1] *Young children in brief separation, no. 3, John,* James and Joyce Robertson, Tavistock Child Development Research Unit 1969

understand.' He was very grateful to the psychiatrist who had recognized the severity of his illness and had secured treatment for him. He has now had a further regression, and is beginning to evolve.

I have spoken about 'context profiles'. I am now going to quote from a Mulberry Bush profile at some length, because this profile concerns another child called Joseph at the age of eleven; in the course of treatment in a therapeutic school he has evolved from a devastating, frozen delinquent to a caretaker-self syndrome, and in such a conscious way that he has been able to report on the process. We have often had referrals who have turned out to be 'caretakers', but this is the first time that we have been able to recognize the formation of the syndrome as it was happening, at such a late age.

My description of a frozen child in Chapter 9 of *Therapy in Child Care* is quoted on p. 99.

One such child was Joseph. At one time we really wondered whether we could continue to contain Joseph in the Mulberry Bush. It seemed to us, at the end of two years' work, that no basic evolvement was taking place, despite carefully planned provision of primary experience by the treatment team. A description of Joseph on referral *still* seemed only too valid at this point. After much discussion, however, we decided to struggle on for a little longer, knowing that if nothing could be achieved, he would certainly become a criminal.

The first sign that I could see of change was Joseph's initial use of symbols. He came to see me, and in the course of a session he communicated for the first time in a symbolic way. A little later it became clear that he was now capable of experiencing a sense of personal guilt, and as one would expect, this achievement brought with it the possibility of depression, and dependence of an early kind.

He came one day for a session. We played 'squiggles' together as usual. I had written his name in full at the top of the first piece of paper: under this he wrote 'JO' within a circle, carefully drawn. This was the first intimation of the presence of his little self–not that I recognized this at the time.

Joseph began gradually to talk of Jo. He told me that little Jo was the size of his thumb, that he constantly was trying to escape and get into mischief, that Joseph had to keep a firm hold on little Jo's hand, because he would run away. He said: 'Jo has to be fed an awful lot, and he needs a long time in the bath. I must always know where he is. He ran away once when he had the nightmare. He's a day older than me–that's how he knew I'd be born. That's how he looked out into the future. He looked out ahead of life. He knew what was coming but he didn't tell me. I'd have been scared, wouldn't I...? Jo had a dream once about ghosts–the ghost chased him out of my bedroom, so for one minute he wasn't with me, so he almost died of horror. We need each other.'

On another occasion, Joseph was riding on Roger Matthew's back.

R.*M.*   You talked about teeth again.
J.   Yes (it's the same).
R.*M.*   The time before was in your bedroom.
J.   That was when the room exploded.
R.*M.*   Because your vest wasn't folded the right way.
J.   *(Tape not clear at this point).*
R.*M.*   When the vest was folded neatly it was alright.
J.   When it wasn't folded–that was bad–that was the wrong way.
R.*M.*   It was crumpled and mixed up.
J.   That was the bad way, that's why the room would explode.
R.*M.*   Does it work just with your vest?
J.   It's just this vest I've got on, it's a magic vest. *(Pulls it out.)*
R.*M.*   I see.
J.   It's just this vest, it's a bit broken.

We discussed this material about Joseph's vest in a context profile. There was a great deal of discussion in the course of this profile, so I have only time to select a few passages from it.

Myself: I am awfully interested about the vest. I've thought and thought about it because it's turned up other times and I've come to the conclusion that the vest is Joseph's description of Freud's barrier against stimuli; his whole way in which he describes the vest suggests that the vest is a protection from impingement: you notice it is so important that it's folded in the right way, and he says 'It's a magic vest' and 'It's a bit broken.' And one would assume from this bit 'It's a bit broken' that this

74

means he has not got something sufficiently protective between him and the outside world; this is not defence in the ordinary sense—a barrier against stimuli is something that Freud described as being provided by the mother and by the environment to protect the baby from impingement—he didn't put it quite like that, but he *did* talk about a barrier against stimuli, and that if this is broken through then there is a lack of a normal protective area, which is actually needed. This comes in very much with frozen children: they simply haven't got a barrier against stimuli, they merge, they haven't got an edge to themselves; they haven't got this barrier which separates them from outside —invasion, impingements, attack, breaking-in—however you like to think of it; and Joseph's use of the vest and the way he speaks about the vest suggests this to me—it's a rather interesting piece of description, the feeling that there is something of this sort that he knows he needs and hasn't really got, so he has a magic vest: but it's broken, it's not really adequate, it doesn't really work—and I am sure it doesn't.

John Armstrong: I am sure that this vest is significant for him; nevertheless, vests are not things that he looks after: he will treat a vest as he treats all his other clothes—he will throw them about. In addition to this it would be interesting to know, if this is so, what sort of climate he was experiencing when he spent so much time getting rid of this vest and not wearing it, when he should be wearing it.

Myself: Well, this would absolutely fit (I didn't know this about Joseph and his vest), in that frozen children don't want such a barrier. When they are really at their illest they want no barrier, they want nothing that prevents them merging with the environment: their aim is re-establishing symbiosis; so, of course, they are not looking for a barrier against stimuli, they use merger instead, in which there is no question of boundaries, or edges or barriers of any kind, and they are terrified by barriers, and panic when barriers are imposed—in other words what we would call imposing boundaries, on such a person, produces panic for this reason.

Douglas Hawkins: Would the vest be symbolic, then?

Myself: Yes. I was simply thinking that he is using this as a symbolic realization, of which he is perfectly capable: I know, because of other material he's produced, and one would be expecting him to achieve symbolization at this point: there's plenty of it in this material, and there's plenty of it in lots of other material which he is producing now; and at this stage one would expect symbolization. In fact this road is well charted, isn't it? One can look out for things and hope to find them at certain stages: it is usually a question of whether one is in a position to see them or not—whether they do become apparent or not. This is not just Joseph, this is any such child at such a stage. It could be anything in Joseph's case; at the moment it is chance, I think, that he chooses the vest for this piece of description, but it is next to his skin, and so when it's not there it *is* there, is my guess now—you know, that he feels there is a vest next to his skin, he feels there's something, there is a protective barrier that is between him and the outside, that he has got a container, there is something that contains him—and he's got an inside and an outside.

D.H. Is this something that's growing?

Myself: Yes, that's right, and consciousness of the existence of Jo, for example, would make this very distinct: the outside world would be looking after the inside.

SECOND EXTRACT

J.A. More and more, I think there's good value for us in continuing this discussion.

Myself: Well, he represents such a lot, doesn't he? He's a very representative person and he's in a process, so that—in a sense —one is able to see what's happening. I've discussed him from time to time with various people who have been working with him, so I've heard a lot about Joseph.

J.A. We really didn't get much past the 'Last Will and Testament' and there is a great deal besides that.

Myself: I've got my own notes on a session I had with Joseph and I would like to discuss these at some point.

R.M. I think I discussed this with you once—in Brian's room there is a chest of drawers and one drawer has been taken out—

Myself: Of course! I remember.

R.M. —and he said 'This is like a mouth', and I didn't understand that, so I let him go on, and I finally realized that it was like a row of teeth with one missing: he then went on to ask me about whether teeth grew again, and I said that only one set of teeth grow again, and that they don't carry on growing.

J.A. Was this recently?

Myself: No, quite a time back, but we had forgotten about it.

R.M. About three weeks after I came.

Myself: I remember clearly, you telling me about it, and how interesting it was because one could see just how he would feel: it looks so like a hole, where a drawer is taken out of a chest of drawers.

R.M. This is a little drawer, as well.

Myself: Yes. You know, one could so easily say 'Well, aren't these castration anxieties?' but my own feeling is that this isn't about this at all, but it is something much more basic and much more to do with the self and identity, and gaps, and all this; so that one could make a mistake...except, that, of course, it could be things at two levels. Could I discuss the notes on my session with Joseph at this point? It wasn't, in a way, a very valuable session for me, but there was very interesting material in it all the same. This was his first squiggle, what he made of it, he said was a house. I said, 'Whose?' and he said, 'Mine'. *Me:* 'What do you do in it?' *Joseph:* 'I stay up to midnight, two nights a week.' *Me:* 'What about the lines all over the house?' *Joseph:* 'The lines are the bricks.' (Then Joseph sort of stopped.) *Me:* 'What do you do in the house?' *Joseph:* 'I play all sorts of games–Lotto, and things like that.' He then drifted off and there wasn't really very much to it. This is the second squiggle, and Joseph said, 'It is a pattern of a star, it reminds me of Apollo 8...9...10.' *Me:* 'Could that be three years of your life?' *Joseph:* 'Ummm . .' *Me:* 'You've been some pretty big journeys in the last three years.' (Really, I was thinking of when he talked about the stages and the phases, earlier.) *Joseph:* 'I've been to Paddington and I've been to . . .' He took this up at a reality level. I didn't want to drift off into this sort of thing, so I asked whether Jo also went on journeys to Paddington and things like that. Joseph has spoken of Jo to me quite often, so this was appropriate. *Joseph:* 'He went to the seaside without me when I was asleep at night: he's always going. In the daytime he climbs trees, sometimes with me, and sometimes without; he always goes on walks with me, I always hold his hand in case he runs away, and of course he sleeps with me. He was ten on Christmas day.' I rather missed out on this one because this would be Jesus, presumably, and Jo... and all sorts of associations ... could be.

J.A. You know that this is Joseph's birthday?

Myself: Oh no, I didn't know anything of the sort. Well, this explains that one–I had forgotten all about Christmas Day being his birthday: this couldn't be simpler, this being the case. Then this was the third squiggle. *Joseph:* 'A fat person: that's what Jo looks like with his disguise, but much smaller, he's only so big in real life' (indicating with his thumb). Here again, I thought this could so easily be a reference to his penis–his thumb and little Jo could be his penis, and this is not at all unusual, and could be the kind of thing that would turn up. Then I thought something that I had not really thought clearly before: when you get symbolization taking place, the last thing one wants to do is to interpret it, because one is only setting the child back to where he was before he symbolized; there's no reason to interpret, it is the last thing you'd think of doing. And, really, I thought it quite probable that the penis represents Jo, rather than that Jo represents the penis.

J.A. Yes, and this made me suddenly think of Julian and his little bear stuck down the front of his trousers.

Myself: Yes, exactly. One could make a great mistake by seeing this the wrong way round; that it really matters an awful lot which way round it is, and one would have to think awfully carefully and watch the material that emerged about this. I was thinking about other material which could point in the same direction, which was why I was thinking about this business of castration fears and so on, and why I was saying it needn't be castration fears, it could be fears for little Jo, who could be represented by his penis, but the basis is there for identity, and himself. And this is where, I think, a lot of people go frightfully wrong... . I'm still a bit confused about it myself, but I think it makes sense. Then Joseph went on: 'Connie still gives me money–half for Jo and half for me.'

J.A. Usually it's two sixpences.

Myself: Well, there you are, and it absolutely fits the material.

Joseph said, 'Same with dinner . . . I bet he won't like the pudding and I'll have to eat both.' This struck me as in a way terribly funny, because of the obvious complications of such a situation – and he went on to say how much Jo likes custard and he doesn't – so Jo can have all the custard. The amount of planning that must go into this! Then Joseph said of Jo, 'He ate my sleeve and made a big hole in it.' Now, isn't there a hole in the vest? I rather wondered whether this was Jo from inside or impingement from outside, or a mixture of both – I just couldn't decide. Joseph, continuing, said '. . . . and my trousers, he makes holes in my blankets and sheets.' *Me:* 'It sounds as though he needs to bite a lot.' *Joseph:* 'Yes, *he does*. I used to hit him a lot, I don't now, I hardly ever hit him now.' That's the lot. It's interesting, isn't it?

THIRD EXTRACT

J.A. I was just thinking, upstairs there must be some forty-five records, and there is only one without a centre, and this is Joseph's, and it's the only record he has, as far as I know. I put it on last and it's quite a job because it doesn't sit on to the thing and you have to get it just right or it goes into orbit, and, of course, it *would* be Joseph's. *He* didn't make an enlarged hole, he did a swop with somebody for it and it had this hole before he came by it.

Myself: Really, it's extraordinary, isn't it? They link up so relevantly, don't they? I was thinking about the hole, and his mouth and the teeth, and Jo, and the possibility of something Winnicott described a long time ago about a child who had emotionally lost his mouth, and we discussed this in terms of a deprived child: at that time, he ate and spoke and so on, but in fact he didn't feel as though he had got a mouth.

J.A. It might as well have been a tube, or something.

Myself: That's right. It had to do with his mother's breast, that there had to be a breast for him to have a mouth, and that is what had been missing – there hadn't been the breast for his mouth, so the mouth didn't come alive.

J.A. Well, there was no demand for it, was there?

Myself: One wonders whether there is something like this here. Wait a minute, there's a little bit in my notes on Joseph's session: here it is, I did miss out a little. Joseph said of Jo: 'He eats more than me. I look after him quite well but we're not always the same, when I'm happy he's often sad.' Then Joseph gave that manic grin at me (you all know the one), and went on, 'now you can see I'm happy, but you can't see him, can you?'

J.A. That's marvellous, isn't it!

Myself: I replied, 'I only know what you tell me about Jo.'

J.A. Joseph is one of the children who will ask for more food, an extra helping, knowing in advance that he won't eat it. And it seems to me that this might be Jo's portion, or to make sure that Jo has enough.

It may well have been difficult to follow this discussion, but I feel that it is of value especially because of Joseph and Jo, and also since it gives some kind of picture of a treatment team reporting in this particular way.

The question now is, will Joseph have a regression, in which he would hand over the care of little Jo to us; or will he continue to be a caretaker-self. Is this as far as he can go? Ideally, we would want him to have a regression, so that Jo could grow up and become Joseph, one whole person. Joseph himself claimed recently that Jo is growing.

My last piece of material concerns Robert, in the Cotswold Community, at the age of fifteen.

Robert was referred to me within the Community because people were worried about him. He came quite willingly, shy, evasive, but friendly. He said, 'Well, what shall we talk about, now I'm here?' I said, 'I thought we might talk about you, Robert.' 'Oh,' he replied, 'there are two of those.' His tone was almost casual. I suggested in an equally calm and commonplace way that he should tell me a bit about *both of them*. He went on to explain that there was the Robert whom I could see and talk with, but also there was the other one—a little boy about eight years old, always getting into mischief. He described how difficult he found the task of controlling the little one. As far as he knew, there had always been the two of them —the little one was delinquent and got very excited: the big one was quiet, shy and withdrawn. Robert said: 'What worries me is that I'll soon be leaving here, and imagine the other one getting out at home or at work. There's nothing I can do for him–I've wondered about a youth club, but they don't *play*, not his way, just games and all that.' I could only sympathize: how could he have a regression at this point? How could he hand over the care of the little one–so much younger than eight years old–to us? Robert said, hesitatingly: 'I've had one idea. Do you think when I'm older and can get married, that my wife would look after him?' I said that this was a real possibility, that many marriages work on this sort of basis, but that it would be important to let the girl know about his little self before they were married. He agreed, and we talked round this.

On a later occasion, he told me, 'I've decided to get rid of him' (the little self), 'I'd get on better without him.' I begged him not to do this: I pointed out that he was talking about destroying his real self. He said, 'I can't keep him any longer.'

He did not want to see me again for some weeks. Then he asked to do so. This time he talked about leaving the Community, and described his mixed feelings. Just as he was going, he exclaimed, 'All the same, if I had a son of my own in trouble, I'd want him to come here.'

My object in putting together this patchwork has been to underline the terrifying fact that unless suitable treatment can be provided, a syndrome of deprivation is unlikely to alter. So a sixteen-year-old can continue to live exactly as he did at the age of two. One could make a similar patchwork from any of the syndromes of deprivation which I have listed. Such a child can be passed from person to person, from place to place, actually conscious of his needs but unable to communicate. This tragedy is not inevitable: we are being given the chance to do something about it.

7
Students with special needs,
1970

I read this to a child care group at Westcliff-on-Sea who brought to the subject a great deal of experience and thought. It seems to me important to realize and accept that many young people, although they may have considerable emotional problems, may with support have a lot to offer in the field of child care.

One could say with truth that every student has special needs, some of which we can meet, others which must be firmly handed back to the student; others, again, which do not surface, concerning which we may speculate, but about which we might not choose to communicate to the student for various good reasons. It is this last category which I am going to consider in this paper, because students with such needs are often precisely the borderline people about whom one asks oneself, 'Should they be coming into the field of child care?' 'Helping other people to help us', chapter 8 in *Therapy in Child Care,* was an attempt to describe the problems which inevitably turn up during supervision, and which really do stem from the students' own needs, rather than from other sources.

I am troubled by the split between experience and conceptualization, which tends to result from periods of practical work followed or preceded by study. Ideally, in this field, I would like to see experience followed by realization leading *at once* to communication and subsequent conceptualization—all taking place in the same place within the student's working day, within the context, in fact. The 'special needs' which I am thinking about would be more readily recognized, I believe, in these circumstances. Perhaps, however, we can approximate to such a way of working, within the framework of the student's supervision during placement—this is a diagnostic opportunity in terms of *need assessment*. Students are going to become staff: just as children need to be diagnosed on a basis of need, so do staff. There has to be an emotional economy in a place, and resources for provision must not be squandered.

As I see it, we have no right to expect students (or ourselves, for the matter of that) to have no special emotional needs, however minimal: but equally, we must be able to recognize and estimate emotional cost to others having to meet such needs—not only colleagues, but also children, however indirectly. This cost has got to be balanced realistically against the contribution such a person may be able to make to the life and work of the total group in a residential place. I am not saying that the more disturbed a student may be the greater will be the strain on the group potential for meeting needs. This is not necessarily so, since many very disturbed people may be highly organized and defended, so that, in a dreadful way they have no conscious needs and make no demands on others. (Indeed, often such apparently self-contained young people are envied by others, and their illness remains unrecognized until serious breakdown takes place.) There are many more obviously disturbed students who, one can see, will present many difficulties and whose needs must be met wherever they may be; who, all the same, have gifts and skills and whose insight may be of value. These are the borderline cases to which I have referred.

What should we as supervisors say to such people? How do we help them, advise them, and report on them to others? Very often these disturbed—but probably valuable—students are themselves emotionally deprived: something has gone wrong at the beginning of their lives, so that they have not had enough experience as babies to build adequate *selves*. In other words there will be gaps in their experience which have left gaps in their ego-functioning. The only treatment which can be of use to any such deprived person is provision of primary experience, either in the course of their lives through deep and dependent personal relationships, or through actual therapeutic treatment (very difficult to obtain). Now, I am not suggesting for a moment that we should provide such treatment for students, nor that we should hope that their needs can be met in this way as staff in child care units; although this may well be the student's own not so unconscious hope, and this hope may have a lot to do with motivation in his or her wish to work in the field of child care. It may, however, be worth while to consider the possibility of planning support for this kind of person, by conscious supplementation of functioning in those areas where the student's ego is missing or inadequate.

I remember one such student, working in a therapeutic school for several months: this was a very gifted and intelligent girl, well qualified and with considerable experience (on an advanced course in the United States). Jane was in most ways an ideal student, of whom we all had a high opinion and whom we respected. From time to time, however, perhaps once in two weeks, Jane would fail to get up in the morning, and would spend the day in bed: on the following morning she would reappear, with a graceful apology for her absence–but no explanation! You will know the irritation and resentment this sort of phenomenon can arouse –Jane's very lack of guilt and anxiety made matters worse. I was fairly certain that these days in bed were in fact 'mini-breakdowns' into regression, really needed by Jane and therefore not a matter of conflict for her. On the other hand, Jane was exploiting others in a split-off sort of way, which enabled her to avoid personal communication and personal responsibility for her survival technique. Obviously this was the tip of an iceberg, and something so well established that change of pattern was not likely to take place without tremendous emotional upheaval. Jane to some extent counted on collusive anxiety among her colleagues: the fear of losing her very real contribution could induce them to close their eyes to her 'departures'.

Following thought and consultation with the team of the therapeutic school, I decided to talk about this problem in its manifest form with Jane. The latent form would be dangerous for anyone of us to approach–it would open up the whole area of her early deprivation, of which we knew nothing. So I talked to Jane about the *reality* of her need to have these days in bed, making it clear to her that I completely accepted the subjective reality of this need. I said all this, sitting on her bed, on such a day. I felt as though I was going through a sound barrier, and expected a sonic boom: she certainly felt threatened and resentful, but my acceptance of the reality of her need gave her some assurance. By *manifest* content of non-functioning areas, I mean what one can see in objective reality: Jane really objectively stayed in bed. The *latent* content of this behaviour would be the *meaning* of staying in bed, for her, deeply rooted in her unconscious, and only to be reached in a treatment setting. Nothing would be more dangerous than interpretation of the need, even supposing the interpretation might be correct. A communicated recognition of the need is a very different matter, and can even be eventually of therapeutic value.

I stressed to Jane that I recognized her need to go to bed on certain days, but also that I felt this must be communicated to others, to be considered as a practical problem requiring a solution. I said that eventually she might not need this withdrawal, but that in the meantime this was something with which she and all of us must live. She claimed that she had never talked about this before, and that others had not challenged her right to withdraw. I assured her that this right was not being challenged, but that plans must be made, communication must be established so that other people could and would—consciously and willingly—stand in for her. In the end, such arrangements were made: the other members of the team were much less resentful in response to Jane's less defended position. Jane herself began consciously to accept the split-off 'gap' as being in herself, in so far that she could accept responsibility for her withdrawals and became able to communicate such a state of non-functioning as soon as she reached awareness of an impending breakdown. Although she was unable to alter this pattern, she became much more conscious of it, so that shortly before her placement came to an end, she could discuss the possibility of telling future employing agencies about the problem—as she would do, after all, if she suffered from severe attacks of asthma. Many people, of course, achieve the same results as Jane, quite unconsciously, through some psychosomatic symptom, which is unlikely to be challenged by others as an escape route.

I do not feel that such steps should be taken by us unless we are confident that the student can offer so much to the place that he or she is *worth* this considerable trouble. We must, however, bear in mind the fact that many apparently down-to-earth sensible students have made a 'flight to reality', and are consequently quite out of touch with their own inner reality and unable to gain real insight; they are unable to achieve empathy with children or grown-ups.

Other deprived students may appear to function successfully, but are in fact delinquent. Delinquency is not so easy to recognize when there is no obvious stealing or other dishonest behaviour. Delinquent personalities can hide behind competence and charm: gradually one starts to feel uneasy. Children are seduced by such a person; grown-ups are manipulated. There is often a paranoid attitude, linked with pairing: this sort of pairing is really merger.[1] The delinquent student merges with a suitable unintegrated child −a host, as it were−and takes up an isolated position with the child *against* the rest of the grown-ups, children in the group. It is my view that no such student should remain in the field of child care. There is nothing to gain by trying to help this kind of person in a unit. I would ask for his or her removal, giving my reasons. It is most unlikely that a delinquent grown-up will evolve, because there are too many secondary gains from delinquency. Some agency must deal with his problem, but *not* the staff of a unit caring for deprived children−*we* cannot meet his needs.

Another deprivation syndrome which I have met among students is the kind of intellectually brilliant person who has had to use his intellect as a defence against his emotional life. Such a person is usually omnipotent and narcissistic, sure of his ability to solve any problem by intellectual means, and consequently scornful of intuition and insight (I am inclined to think of insight as informed intuition). This kind of student is a constant source of irritation to all: his sheer intellectual ability can be a threat, and his ability to argue himself out of untenable positions by the use of rather dotty logic can be actually destructive. This student certainly has special needs, of which he is usually unaware because of massive defences. The supervision of such a student can be utterly exhausting and frustrating, unless one takes measures from the first to control the situation. I personally, as soon as I recognize an extreme intellectual defence, insist from the first on basing all discussion on the student's actual experiences in the place. Here again, I do not interpret, except once removed, as it were: in the material which emerges the student will probably be able to stand some gain of insight. This kind of person may be deeply concerned for the children in the place, and even relatively free emotionally in regard to them, but the intellectual defence will be mobilized

---

[1]I use the word 'merger' to describe a symbiotic bond, where one person merges with another, or a group, in order to escape responsibility of identity.

against parental figures or in sibling rivalry. Providing that insight can be gained gradually, and the supervisor is not trapped into a punitive attitude, such a student can continue to evolve into a successful worker.

So far I have been talking for the most part about endemic pathological states in students. There can be special needs which are occasional emergencies and which need to be met at once: for example, shock. It is not unusual for a student, especially in a unit catering for disturbed children or adolescents, to be sailing along quite successfully as far as we can see, only to break down in one way or another at the end of a few weeks. Usually warm concern and support are all that is needed, with opportunities for communication. I have found it useful to warn students of this possibility of stress. Sometimes such a breakdown is not only shock, but an uncovering of deep disturbance, triggered off by reflection in the children. There can, however, be pockets of disturbance in people which are usually fairly well insulated, and the same approach as for shock can re-establish the necessary defences. On the whole, I do not, as a supervisor, encourage students to talk about their own personal lives, but there should be a time and a place for this when they need urgently to communicate something to us about themselves, often on a basis of trust in our reliability in regard to the children. Therapeutic listening with a minimum of comment can be a kind of first aid at these moments.

If one finds that a student is quite unable to cope emotionally in some specific area—for example, the management of panic in children—I would suggest that, rather as with non-functioning areas, we accept the reality of this specific inability, communicate our acceptance to the student, and see to it that he is not expected to manage such situations except in a secondary role.

You will realize that I am thinking here about students who are not fully integrated as individuals. These are the ones with the really special needs: they can be valuable workers eventually, but in the meantime they can only too easily collect the roles of proteges or scapegoats. I have met them in every area of caring for children. Their gifts arouse envy and their underfunctioning arouses resentment, but some of them can do valuable work; and in all of them is the potential to evolve.

8
Need assessment – I
Finding a basis, 1970

The Home Office asked me to run a workshop on need assessment–from dawn till dusk!–at Bournemouth, as part of a course for experienced workers. This was an immensely stimulating and exciting experience, and we were all exhausted by the end of it! There have been several workshops on need assessment since this first one, including an occasion when Barbara Chumbley and I worked together with a course over two days.

The notes which follow are written from a highly personal point of view, and from a position outside the field of child care. I could have attempted to make some sort of survey of means of assessment that are in use here and in other countries. I could have advocated this method and deprecated that; wished for this or that sociometric scale; or groaned over some projection technique: what I have actually done is to make basic assumptions to assume that any human being making an assessment of the state of any other human being is faced inevitably by the same difficulties within himself, whatever techniques are employed in the task of assessment. Just at the moment, so much is in a state of flux: presently, no doubt our work will reset into various stereotyped forms. But here and now, there is an element of choice, just because there is also an element of uncertainty. We are thinking today especially about the problems attending assessment at the point of taking into care. Perhaps the 'winds of change' are even altering the meaning of 'care'.

The word 'assessment' has a final ring; there is something absolute about the statement or series of statements which may alter the entire life of an individual human being. Those people who make assessments are in an omnipotent position: how they move and countermove will depend on many factors–and ultimately the arrangements of their words written on paper will tend to lead to instant action, since in the circumstances, if such action were not needed there would not be in the first place a request for an assessment. In other words, the process of assessment is usually required to deal with crisis. The action necessary (whatever this may be) results from a state of emergency in the life of a person within a group. You will have noticed that, so far, I have not used the word 'child'. I think I am especially anxious that we should be thinking of a *person* who is a child; who was a baby and who will become a grown-up, but who throughout all his life should be respected as a person. In this connection, I was considering the word 'pity' recently and wondered why I dislike the sound of 'pity': I concluded that 'pity' is not a feeling which of necessity involves 'respect'. I found myself preferring 'compassion', which—for me, anyhow—implies respect for the human being who evokes my compassion. 'Pity' has overtones of patronage—it comes from above, downwards. You will realize that I am wondering about the attitudes which various workers must bring to the task of assessment. I am remembering a report made by an army psychiatrist on a seven-year-old boy who had caused a lot of trouble: in this report the psychiatrist described the child as 'a potential psychopath' and I am asking myself whether he really thought about the possible effect of such a dangerous and final assessment on the rest of the boy's life.

A fifteen-year-old was sent to an approved school from a classifying school. He was described as a case of school truancy. I read the various reports and recommendations, dating from when he was seven years old. His elder brother had been murdered in Orchard Street—this was stated in one report. In another report his truancy was described: this had started when he was seven, and the school from which he played truant was the 'Orchard Street School'. *No connection* in all the intervening years had been made by the reporting agencies between the street in which his brother was murdered, and the school *in the same street* from which he fled. Nevertheless, all the information was there, clearly to be read in the two separate reports, linking the murder with what was, of course, an unrecognized school phobia. Here at least were clues which could eventually be found which helped us to assess the boy's final state. Often, however, there are no real facts available, either because those people from whom we are trying to collect information are inadequate or because they really do not know what happened during the critical years of the child's early child-hood. A boy of about eight who was coming to see me from time to time, wondered about the curious pock marks which covered his face. Eventually he and I realized that these must have been self-inflicted, in the course of terrible deprivation in early child-hood. It was not until much later that we found confirmation (through a chance meeting with a nurse): for months, as a toddler, he had torn at his own face with his fingernails. The pock marks were there for all to see, but there was no mention of this evidence of despair in any of the detailed reports. Parents, teachers and others are often themselves in the whirlpool of the crisis, full of guilt and anxiety, which made their reporting highly subjective.

I remember how, long ago, a little boy was referred to the Mulberry Bush by a child guidance clinic. He was described by his mother as violent and dangerous: she gave detailed descriptions of his disturbed behaviour and eventually he was sent to us, having formally been ascertained maladjusted. Actually it was soon clear that he was indeed a very disturbed child, although we were puzzled by the fact that he did not present the behaviour pattern drawn in such detail by his mother. At a later stage when I took this up with her one day, she suddenly revealed to me that she had been describing her husband's behaviour at home: it seemed to her that only by attaching this to her little son could she report her husband's maladjustment without disloyalty to him!

With the decrease in the number of court orders, the positions and attitudes of parents of delinquent children may be radically altered. We can hope that parents will become less guilty and anxious, and consequently less defended, so that they may be free to consider their own and their children's problems more objectively with us, provided that we can give them adequate support.

In order to make any kind of assessment in regard to a person, information must be collected by other people from other people and then communicated by people to people. This final communication is bound to be influenced by all the current factors operating in the lives of the many people involved – above all, by the sense of urgency, because of the 'crisis' climate of which I have already spoken. All the *feelings* of the worried people engulfed in the crisis, are going to be in the assessment and also all the feelings of the workers who are making the assessment

There is a famous French film about this problem, concerning the jury in a murder trial–a study of the effects of their current problems on their judgment. The parents (if there are parents) will be trying to deal with guilt and inadequacy. The workers may be feeling a different sort of guilt, if they are in fact having to take a child away from his home and family–however inadequate these may be.

There will be the feelings evoked by the child's personality in those who are dealing with him at such a moment, and also *his* reaction to the strangers who have come into his life which will affect his behaviour. Given such an emotional climate, it may be difficult to sort out the objective reality. The history presented by the parents may omit much, and distort even more (for example, the mother of battered babies). The child may present a false picture of himself, because he will be under great stress: even his intelligence may be blurred by underfunctioning due to emotional disturbance. A disturbed boy of high average intelligence was involved in a delinquent act which brought him before a magistrate's court. He was retested at this point (at the request of the magistrate) and his intelligence now appeared to be well below average at 80. A year later, by which time he had started to respond to treatment, his good intelligence was, on further testing, once again in evidence.

Of course, in a reception centre much of this confusion can be to some extent sorted out; but even here the child may not be able to communicate his needs and his real personality, either by what he says or what he does.

I think we are accepting too easily a process of a structured kind, which gives everyone concerned the illusion of solving problems and making appropriate recommendations, when actually we may not have reached the real problems; and our recommendations–however appropriate–may be impossible to implement. I am in favour of communicating and tolerating doubt: it is rare in assessments–of disturbed children, for example– to meet words like 'possibly', 'perhaps', 'we think', or even 'we do not understand'.

Most of my experience of assessments has been of those made by child guidance clinic teams and these are usually excellent valid reports, but even such highly professional teams–who may not be working in a crisis climate—can make mistakes. For example: a frozen delinquent boy was referred to us as 'deeply depressed'. Within a few months there was dramatic evidence that the so-called depression was only a state of hibernation between one delinquent explosion and the 'next, which suddenly took place for all to see. His delinquent exploits had up till this point escaped discovery. I believe that such mistakes are inevitable; that no reporting can be entirely objective, and that the information collected in a situation of stress may well be invalid; but I am not supposing for a moment that we can *avoid* error, that we can ever be sure that we are making a correct assessment of a breakdown in a constellation of lives. I am only urging that we should support each other in the toleration of doubt, and recognize the inadequacy of the knowledge on which we must depend in order to take action which will affect the future life of the person concerned to an extent which we are in no position to calculate.

What will be the population of a community home? How are we going to judge whether such placement will meet the needs of *this* child at *this* time? What can such a home offer? Are we able to classify children in such a way that, in taking them into care for the first time we can ensure that they will be obtaining *appropriate* care? Some of you may have seen the devastating Robertson film called '*John*,'[1] in which a normal integrated toddler is placed by his father in a residential nursery, in a group of institutionalized little children who are cared for by young nursery nurses working on a shift system. By the end of seventeen days John is destroyed by his environment, perhaps never to recover. The caring was in itself kind, but ill-planned and inadequate; nevertheless the same standard of care in a group of integrated toddlers would not have been so disastrous (this placement was, of course, planned by the parents). Are we going to be able to *plan* emotional environments or shall we in the event, like John's father, have to use whatever place we can find?

I feel we should be able to decide whether we are going to mix integrated and unintegrated children in one living group, or whether we may plan in such a way as to have integrated groups

[1] See footnote p. 72.

and unintegrated groups, with two distinct kinds of provision based on need. I realize that decisions will rest with the social workers and the children's department: even a case which comes before the magistrates will return to the children's officer. Up till now, the decision as to whether a delinquent boy would go to an approved school or a school for the maladjusted often depended on the particular views of a probation officer. Who will now decide his placement, and on what basis? What specialized knowledge will immediately be available to a children's department? Will there be enough consultation available with the responsible key people in the child's life–the teacher, the general practitioner, the health visitor? How much time will be available to consider the doubtful cases–whether or no to take a little child into care? Often there will not be much room for doubt, but it must sometimes be difficult to decide: who, exactly, will reach this decision? Suppose that an unintegrated aggressive boy goes into a reception home, unable to make relationships: will he meet there normal children awaiting appropriate placement? What will be the effect on the normal, integrated children, who will be distressed and vulnerable in any case because of a strange environment?

You will understand that I know very little about the actual process of taking a child into care: there may be immediate answers to my questions. But perhaps questions which have been answered in one context may be asked again in another, even though the original answers may still turn out to be valid. Certainly, in the field of residential placement of maladjusted children, I have the feeling that placement in a school is too often the discovery of a vacant place, rather than the meeting of the needs of the particular child and the matching of child to school. This is not a criticism of assessment, there is an inevitable collusion of which we are all to some extent guilty, in which we *accept* that something actually essential is not available, and assess accordingly; for example, –the fact that there are not enough adolescent units. I would hope that we are free to insist that assessment and recommendation should have in mind *what is needed* over and above *what is available*.

Perhaps the community homes will be able to provide a considerable variety of provision around a campus: a flexible range which will enable a child to move from one unit to another on a basis of need fulfilment. For example: an 'intensive care' unit in terms of emotional provision might be able to give treatment (primary provision) to a child for a comparatively short period, followed by skilled but less intensive care in a more normal environment.

Since need assessments were first introduced in the Mulberry Bush and the Cotswold Community we have taken a further step and are now evolving a referral need assessment made by the referring agency (a classifying school, reception centre, or whatever) in communication with the placement under conisderation.

It would seem that we can never assess need sufficiently early, and rarely under normal conditions. I believe that assessment centres should be run on the lines of day hospitals, with children living in their own homes whenever possible during assessment; we would be much more likely to make accurate assessments in such circumstances. There will, of course, be a considerable difference between a referral need assessment and an ongoing need assessment (which will be one of a series). In both cases all need assessments must, in my view, be made by a group, *never* by an individual collecting information or depending upon interview procedure.

There is a useful word which I have only met as a traffic term, used on main roads: this is the word 'clearway'. I feel that we need a clearway for discussion, without the pressure of crisis, which can so easily force us to reach decisions in assessment which may not be appropriate for this person who is about to become 'a child in care'.

9
Need assessment – II
Making an assessment, 1970

The particular kind of need assessment which I shall be discussing
came into being as the result of a collection of experiences, working
in a consultant role in a school for deeply disturbed and deprived
children (the Mulberry Bush) and in a therapeutic community
which has evolved from an approved school (the Cotswold Community). At the Mulberry Bush I evolved a type of reporting which
I called 'context profiles'.[1] When making a context profile, the
whole team consider one child, chosen by the team, for a week.
Each member describes any actual personal experiences which he
has had with this child: observations are not allowed. I myself
have a therapeutic session with the child concerned during the
week. All notes are brought to the school secretary, who then
types the material and circulates the notes to the team and to me,
so that we can meet at the end of the week to discuss our experiences, drawing conclusions from the material and gearing a
treatment programme to the needs which become apparent.
Donald Winnicott made the valuable comment that, by using this
method, the team can for an instant see the *whole* child, because all
the 'bits' are brought together in the profile – not only the bits of
the child, but also all our feelings about him. Following the dis-

[1] See *Therapy in Child Care*, ch. 10

cussion, all the notes are arranged in a classification on context: thus all 'getting up' experiences are together and 'mealtimes' and 'bedtimes' are treated in the same way. Since each person may have very different experiences, the outcome is a study in depth of the child and ourselves, attempting to avoid the snares of pseudo-objectivity[1].

From the work on one child, light is often thrown on the needs and treatment of others. The context profile discussion is recorded on tape (the notes are typed in advance) and the whole profile is arranged as described, by our secretary, Mrs Connie Barrett. Ultimately we have something valuable both to us, to psychiatrists, and to newcomers to the team. The work, however, is time-consuming and nowadays we decide to do a profile only when we are especially puzzled and concerned about a particular child. I found that in order to make use of a context profile (at a clinic, for example), I needed to make an analysis. This I did by asking myself certain questions, to which I found answers in the material. Working in parallel at the Cotswold Community, I showed the teams of the various houses how to make context profiles. Here there are four teams (instead of one, as at the Mulberry Bush) and very little secretarial help. There is, inevitably, more coming and going of the adolescent delinquents (because of court orders, up to the present) and in any case, I only meet these groups at the Cotswold once weekly, whereas I meet the Bush team twice weekly. All these factors made the task of writing profiles very difficult.

At the Bush selection has always been based on primary deprivation, so that we are carefully selecting unintegrated children for treatment. At the Cotswold referrals are mixed–integrated and unintegrated–with a much larger unintegrated group than we originally realized. We have found that it is essential to classify boys on arrival as integrated or unintegrated as soon as possible, and it was in order to make this possible that I tried to plan a need assessment. I hoped this would categorize, consider the stage of integration reached, and formulate needs and the treatment to meet these needs.

I decided to use exactly the questions which I ask myself when

[1]See chapter 5.

analysing a profile. This meant employing a certain amount of terminology, but I improvised a glossary (I find terms necessary as a kind of shorthand; otherwise one is employing essays instead of terms). I reached the decision to use these particular questions because I had arrived at them through actual relevant experience: in the event, they proved of use. No doubt in time, we may ask some more questions and omit existing ones: the whole idea is still at a workshop stage, but perhaps for that reason it calls for discussion and experiment. We may also find clearer terms, but since these words are the ones which I employ at present, I have let them stand, with explanations.

CLASSIFICATION

The process of arriving at a need assessment is described in detail below. I have tried to approach the problem of meeting the child's needs—whatever these may be—by classification (rather than by considering his symptoms). I think it will always be necessary for a senior worker to lead such a group discussion, asking and explaining the questions, and recording the answers. There can be no 'yes' or 'no' answers: all replies must be based on actual experiences with the child. We have found that this kind of assessment helps us in planning for the child's management and care.

A need assessment in no way replaces other assessments (case history, intellectual ability and so on), but I find it a valuable addition to other information.

The questions in this assessment can only be answered for the first time by a group of people who are living with the child, and have been doing so for at least three or four weeks: they must understand that this is a *first* need assessment—others will be necessary in order to meet the child's evolving needs. Only a group of resident workers can draw on the kind of experience essential to this type of assessment.

The questions may seem odd at first, but they seem to obtain the kind of information necessary, and workers quickly become accustomed to this approach. A need assessment usually takes an hour of group work to complete.

NEED ASSESSMENT

Classification

Is this child integrated as a person, or is he unintegrated? To judge this, one should ask oneself:

(*a*) *Does he panic?* By panic, I mean a state of unthinkable anxiety –almost a physical condition. (Many so-called 'temper tantrums' are panics.)

(*b*) *Does he disrupt?* By this, I mean does he disrupt a group activity or a happening between two other people?

It would appear, from evidence so far, that the presence of panic and disruption fairly frequently in a child's life justifies us in considering him, for the present, as being unintegrated.

If you are sure that panic and disruption are rarely experienced, then go on to the next section, in which the needs of integrated children are considered.

UNINTEGRATED CHILDREN

If he seems to be unintegrated, go on to the next question.

1. *What is the syndrome of deprivation?* This can be judged by answers to the following questions. What is the state of feelings in this child in regard to

(*a*) personal guilt

This refers to concern; to what one could call healthy guilt–not a fear of being punished or found out, but an acceptance of a personal responsibility for harm done to others, of a kind which can lead to making reparation.

(*b*) Dependence on people or a person

(*c*) Merger

This is the way in which some children become merged with one other or with a group (a typically delinquent phenomenon).

(*d*) Empathy

I like to think of this as being a capacity to imagine what it must feel like to be in someone else's shoes, while remaining in one's own.

(*e*) Stress

How does this child appear to deal with feelings of stress?

(*f*) Communication
Does he *really* communicate, or does he just chatter in a sterotyped way?

(*g*) Identification
Does he, for example, seem to model himself on a grown-up he admires, or on another child? Be careful not to confuse this with *merger*.

(*h*) Depression
Is he sometimes very depressed, or is he indifferent, or always apparently cheerful? Is he at times deeply sad? There is a kind of state of low level of consciousness–just 'ticking over'–sometimes even in deprived children, which I call 'hibernation' and which should not be confused with depression.

(*i*) Aggression
–verbal and physical.

2. *What is his capacity for play?*
(*a*) Narcissistic
Does he play a lot alone, with pleasure?

(*b*) Transitional
Does he, for example, make use of a transitional object?

(*c*) Pre-oedipal
Does he usually like to play with one other, usually a grown up?

(*d*) Oedipal
Does he play with more than one grown up at a time?

(*e*) Post-oedipal
Does he play with other children, able to keep rules, and so on?
(See *Therapy in Child Care,* ch. 11.

3. *What is his capacity for learning*–in every sort of learning situation? Does he learn from experience?

4. *What is his capacity for self preservation?* Is he accident prone? Does he take care of himself and his belongings? Does he seem to value himself?

From the material it is usually quite possible to make a good guess at the *stage of integration* reached. The stages are as follows (see *Therapy in Child Care*, pp. 99–101):

(*a*) Frozen
(*b*) Archipelago
(*c*) False-self
(*d*) Caretaker-self

(On this 'inside diagnosis' a need assessment can be made. There is nothing *absolute* about such recommendations; we cannot be certain, but this assessment gives us a foundation for a treatment programme.) In general, one could say that the needs of these categories are as follows:

(*a*) *Frozen*. Containment, especially of self-destructive areas. Mergers to be interrupted.
Delinquent action to be anticipated—essentially, *confrontation in advance*, i.e. knowing what the child is going to do.
Acting out to be converted into communication.
Dependence on grown-ups to be established.
Delinquent excitement to be changed into oral greed.
Depression to be reached, and supported, following a capacity for personal guilt.
Open communication—with one; with others.

(*b*) *Archipelago*. To relate one ego-functioning islet to others, through communication.
Containment of non-functioning areas, e.g. panics.
Support and encouragement of any functioning areas.
Provision of localized regression where needed, with reliable adaptation.

(*c*) *False-self*. Containment of chaos within the shell. Provision of regression, always planned and localized, with reliable adaptation. Symbolic communication.

(*d*) *Caretaker-self*. Provision for localized regression, reached through cooperation with the 'caretaker', in the care of the real self.
Symbolic communication.
Localized adaptations with as much communication as possible between grown-ups and child.
Functioning areas should be strongly backed.

The particular form which such primary provision should take will depend on the personality of the child and on what he indicates, however indirectly. There will need to be *verbal* and *pre-verbal* communication.

There must be reassessment quite frequently—whenever fundamental evolvement is noted, or indeed any real change for better or worse.

Integrated children

Where the original classification indicates that the child is integrated, the position is very different and need assessment is more complex. We can say with certainty, however, that an integrated, neurotic child will need from us:

Ego support, especially where there is under-functioning: e.g. with doubtful, anxious children.
Reliable parental figures, on to whom he can transfer the unresolved conflicts in regard to his parents.
Ways in which he can make positive use of aggression.
'Open' communication, and the opportunities for conversion of acting-out into verbal communication.
Encouragement and opportunity to accept responsibility as an individual in a group (here 'shared responsibility' becomes very important).
Acceptance of reparation, and help to reach this reparation.
Help in modifying a harsh super-ego.

Nevertheless, need assessment for integrated children will be far more individual and must be considered in great detail.

Notes

1. I have considered especially the needs of unintegrated children, because so many of the children we are trying to help are in fact only partially integrated, and these are the ones who present the greatest problems of management.
2. Please bear in mind that this is only an experimental draft which will need to be developed as a result of experience. Suggestions and alterations will be needed.
3. I have said nothing about symptoms, because this fails to reach *needs*. Children come to us because of their needs, not their symptoms.

Here is a need assessment on Lilian, carried out by the Bush team working with me. (At the Cotswold Community, some teams are doing need assessments by themselves, so that we can discuss the material when we meet.)

Classification

Presence of panic and disruption: Both present, therefore *unintegrated*.

1. What is the state of feelings in Lilian in regard to
   (a) *Guilt* (guilt really means concern). There is a capacity for feelings of personal guilt which shows in compunction in regard to wrong or hurtful things which she has done, which does not *seem* to stem from fear of punishment.
   (b) *Dependence* on person or people (this category includes trust). Lilian is able to be dependent on individuals and also is able to be dependent on the Mulberry Bush. (Example: it is not now necessary for her to be sick on returning to the school; she does not have to test all the time, because expectations are established.)
   (c) *Merger*. Yes, she does merge. More with individuals, but ocassionally with the group. One could use the term 'passive merger'—she passively accepts being used.
   (d) *Empathy*. There is a possible capacity for empathy. Sometimes, perhaps, it might be projective identification.
   (e) *Stress*. Under stress, Lilian is liable to break down into states of panic rage, although this is rather less in evidence than at an earlier stage. (When in one of these states she will bite, she will spit—it will be all over her face, she will throw around everything in the room.) She can sometimes contain and communicate stress.
   (f) *Communication*. Lilian is capable of direct communication: at certain stages it is possible for her to communicate even when under stress.
   (Example of direct communication: when the group came back from a school outing, when the children were very tired, Lilian said, 'The trouble is, I hate my sister and she hates me.')

Query as to whether her long monologues are communication or a defence against communication. There is considerable confusion–sometimes there are flights of associations based on the immediate context or environment. Sometimes mode of communication resembles that of one very old.

(g) *Identification.* Her mannerisms, the way she walks, seem very like those of an elderly person. Lilian does not much appear to be identified with people here; identifications (what there are) come from her past and her background, rather than from anything that has happened here.

(h) *Depression.* Very sad a lot of the time: tinged with self-pity. She rather enjoys sorrowful, tearful, woeful things; enjoys the feeling of being sad. (When the saddest things are on television her face is lit up with pleasure!) This is more likely to be primary masochism.

(i) *Aggression.* Her form of movement could be seen as fairly aggressive. Not really aggressive unless provoked–aggression seen in self defence. (Example: Sheila slapped Lilian's face and Lilian called Sheila a 'black bitch', Sheila slapped her face then for this, Lilian again called Sheila a black bitch, and this just went on and on.) Lilian displays a certain courage to the point of living dangerously, but seems quite unaware of her place in the hierarchy of children. The words 'angry' and 'outraged' apply to her attitudes.

2. What is her capacity for play?
Narcissistic; mainly narcissistic, just beginning to be able to play on her own but in a group–but this is still alone.

3. What is her capacity for learning?
She does not seem very able to learn from experience; she cannot avoid disaster even when shown step by step what is going to happen to her; she goes on with her basic assumptions. There is some learning capacity in group: she can do simple sums and write figures, although she is unable to read or write. Although there is some learning capacity for number work, in general she has a very low capacity in all areas. Must take into consideration her low I.Q. and deafness–both of these factors could aggravate this inability to learn. (With very high

motivation, some learning has taken place–she can now decide what she wishes to spend her 5p on in the tuck shop.)

4. What is her capacity for self preservation?
   Lilian shows signs of physical self preservation, but not of emotional self preservation. She does use adults to protect her, is not accident prone.

Stage of integration reached:

False-self. This after much discussion but within the confines of the headings; given, the collected data indicated false-self child, but with some evidence of a real core.

Need assessment recommendation:

We should support any area that is functioning. Containment of chaos within the shell. Provision of regression, always planned and localized, with reliable adaptations. Symbolic communication.

Other recommendations:

This child's I.Q. is so low that this could be the wrong school for her; there is the added problem of her deafness. One cannot overlook, however, that whatever her problems here, they will be equally valid in, say, an E.S.N. school.

The strain, for Lilian, of being here with children of higher intelligence, could be too great and her need could be somewhere where the whole thing would be geared to a lower I.Q. and to her deafness.

Despite the handicaps she has clearly benefited from being here, and it might not be in her best interests to lose what she obviously gains from the Mulberry Bush School and us.

How much regression has Lilian had here, and has she indicated a need for regression? We assume that for a false-self child to recover, there must be regression–they have got to go to bits and then come together and start off again. From the fact that she tries to get in on the act (i.e. wanting to have German measles when Susan had them: saying she had wet the bed, etc.) it could well be that she is looking for some means of regression.

Is Lilian able to indicate adaptations, and are there any available for her? Felt she would like a good adaptation made available: there is quite a bit of regression going on around and she takes full advantage of this.

The position is that is she is going to need a real regression, a lot of adaptation and a lot of very early experience, very definite focused primary provision for quite a time; this would be the only way in which this particular syndrome would evolve: equally, we may feel that this isn't something that we here can provide because of the added factors of the low I.Q. and the deafness, which may make it really impossible, if so, then we will have to think of other placement. If, however, she is to stay here, it could only be on a basis of real regression, and to what extent this is possible, and how, with someone like this, I don't know. One would say the need assessment is adaptation leading to regression with the beginning of integration following: a very big regression and then reforming, not reaching conceptualization (so many children do, after regression)—she would *realize* what she had been through, but she wouldn't be able to *think* it out. But she could make use of a regression.

You may be interested to know that, after the assessment, the team was in a better position to understand and meet Lilian's needs, and progress has been made in her treatment, so that it seems likely that she will stay with us, and that her regression will be reached.

You will notice that the first classification—whether integrated or unintegrated—is made on the presence or absence of panic and disruption. There is a further clue in the question relating to ego functioning, 'Is there a capacity for empathy?' (not to be confused with projective identification). Should one at that point find clear evidence of empathy, one should return to the question of panic and disruption, since it may be, for example, that acute but contained states of anxiety have been mistaken for panic.

You will also have noticed that we are primarily concerned with state of mind rather than behaviour. Symptoms turn up in discussion, but these—especially acting out—are considered as broken-down communications of state of mind; our treatment plans being based on the needs which the broken-down communications indicate.

Of course, in using need assessment within a residential unit, we assume that other appropriate information is already either in our possession, or at least readily available. A series of need assessments *can* only be used in a residential place by a team working together and living with the child. I suspect, from my own experience as a consultant, that a wealth of valuable material is available in any children's home, but that child care workers need a professional structure and discipline in order to communicate and organize reports which will lead to appropriate treatment programmes. This is equally true both in approved schools and in schools for maladjusted children.

Here is another need assessment, on a recovering boy, who was so unintegrated and dangerous on referral that we wondered whether we could hold him. He was on referral what I have termed an 'archipelago' child, who progressed to become a 'caretaker self', and is now precariously integrated. It is very interesting to see phases of development belonging to the first year of life, turning up during treatment.

BRUCE'S NEED ASSESSMENT

Integrated: Perhaps barely. Does not panic (psychotic area could be quite large). Disrupts in a very conscious way.

1. *Ego functioning*
   Feelings of
   (a) *Guilt*. Yes.
   (b) *Dependence*. Yes.
   (c) *Merger*. Very much diminishing—certainly meeting him, one gets a very clear impression of identity.
   (d) *Empathy*. Yes.
   (e) *Stress*. Depends very much on the relationship formed with grown-up with him at particular time. If he meets a stressful situation involving other children, he will now preserve himself: with a grown-up he can on occasions tend to trust in the grown-up to cope with the situation for him.

   More and more, when he is anxious, frightened or angry, this results in an inturned situation where he goes silent (what one could call an 'inplosion') and takes the trouble in with him, then, with encouragement, it comes out with a rush, shouting, i.e. an explosion. (He is further ahead than we could have ever hoped, when we think of all the ghastly things he used to do at the slightest stress.)

(*f*) *Communication.* Pretty good, both verbal and non-verbal: particularly non-verbal. He uses looks as a very conscious tool, gesture—he knows he has an expressive face, and uses it.

(*g*) *Identification.* Yes, in a positive sense. (With his group teacher and with his father, but as two clear and distinct things; he consciously separates group teacher (Brian) and father.)

(*h*) *Depression.* Yes—quite sad. Suggestion that manic flight could come in here, when he throws things, etc., much laughing, all a flight from feeling personal guilt and depression.

(*i*) *Aggression.* Yes. Incident with Bill and a very angry Bruce chasing him with a piece of glass: Robin felt on this occasion that Bruce would have used it if there had not been intervention. Still doubt really as to what Bruce may or may not do—and to what extent intervention on all occasions is justified. (This is a child who has been given cause for murderous rage at home; what this step-mother has made his father into is one of many reasons.) He is still capable of what seems to be less than conscious destruction.

(Comment from myself: A psychotic area of a person is something that is not capable of evolvement. The violent bit of him even might eventually be accepted by him and others as a mad bit, rather than an unintegrated bit.)

He tolerates his step-mother now, for the pleasure of being with his father.

2. What is his capacity for play?
Narcissistic. No longer: does not now play on his own with his soldiers, no longer plays with lots of little pieces but prefers one larger thing—a bike, a gun or a football.
Post-oedipal. Not over good, but he does manage.

3. What is his capacity for learning?
Academic. Had his step-mother not destroyed his pleasure in learning, he would be much more receptive. He could do

with time entirely alone with a teacher, when he is capable of learning a great deal very quickly. One needs to overcome his unpleasant associations with learning, and combine this with skilful teaching and he should flourish.

Reading: reading age has gone up $1\frac{1}{2}$ years in this last year, and 2 years in the previous year.

Numbers: he likes number work and is prepared to do it. He uses it as a medium of identification with his father (who is in electronics). He still has a relatively short attention span, which is a handicap.

Learning from experience. He is wily, aware, and knowledgeable, very quick. An example was concerned with the sheepdog trials at the church fete. Brian set out to explain the routine to Bruce as he might to his own son, who is aged six. Bruce interrupted, saying, 'Don't go on, it's a code.' He can pick up the whole notion or idea immediately–a great capacity for learning.

He provokes other children: he calls it 'starting trouble' I suggested that this is the only way he can get attention from his father at home, by 'starting trouble'. Father appears a very detached man. Feeling is that Bruce can now relate to a man, father is getting a transference as it were; evidence of more warmth from father on recent visit here. So able to communicate with father, and father is able to respond: emotional change in Bruce (rather than maturation) has made this possible. (I recalled the first meeting with Bruce and his father: it was chilling. There was no connection whatever between these two: this great tall man and this tiny little shrivelled up tadpole sitting at some distance from his father; and one couldn't see what on earth they had in connection with each other . . . although his father was concerned, worried about him, wanting to do something.)

4. What is his capacity for self preservation?
Very much more self preservative than he was. This seems to stem from when he deliberately cut himself deeply with a sharp balsa knife. Group teacher would have like to have made it a significant thing but was wary of doing so. When Bruce starts trouble now, it is consistently pointed out that he does more harm to himself than to other people; recently he has been able to say 'Why?' and we are able to go through the things that he

is doing to himself when he started these situations: now he is able to give up with a smile, grin or wink as a communication that he has not finally, irrevocably hurt himself that time. (I wondered if a lot of the going-on was to gain attention.... At one time he may have felt that the only way he could obtain attention from his father, or any man, was to hurt himself; hence his quite terrible accident-proneness when he first came to us. We really felt it was too dangerous for him, for us to keep him here.)

Capacity for self-preservation is now quite good, although there are moments when he contemplates suicide quite consciously: before it was not conscious but was as if something overwhelmed him; so there are still suicidal elements which could come into the mad bit of him. The suicide bit now tends to come when he is depressed or sad: he is fascinated by death. He is attempting to preserve himself, but the battle to maintain himself is great.

There is a refusal to grow, a refusal to get better.

SUMMARY

From the above material this would seem to be a more or less integrated child, with a mad area, who could be left permanently with a suicidal tendency, or a tendency to murder (this would be incredibly impulsive). These are dangers of which he must gradually, as he grows older and stronger, become more aware and be something of which he is conscious and can take precautions against.

The acquisition of knowledge is very important to him and with this he will achieve a great deal in his own eyes: a great boost to his morale. He has an incredible agility of mind.

Felt that if he could win an intellectual argument with his mother, this would make the world of difference to his self-esteem in the home situation: or, if he could teach his mother something (say, chess) and she could stand being taught by him—if this could be 'sold' to her as the most beneficial thing she could do, to allow him to teach her something . . . John doubted that she wanted to do anything beneficial. He has got to be put in a position where he is independent of her from this sort of standpoint, and able to hold his own.

I went through the listed needs of integrated children. Extra comment on 'Help in modifying a harsh super-ego', i.e. help in replacing the punitive super-ego, which he has certainly got, by a more benign one, which one hopes he will incorporate from his experiences with us.

Group teacher commented on his responsibility within group which is showing signs of developing. He was asked by another child in the group what the difference between a Big and a Small was. Bruce's reply was 'a small somebody starts something, and a big somebody stops it'.

About reparation, as this could be important: he will give a grudging 'sorry' with no heart in it whatsoever; there is no evidence that he feels concern.

One of the main things then is to help him to obtain, contain and make use of, as much knowledge as possible as is going to be of use to him in living his life, and to modify the super-ego as far as we possibly can; and to find ways of helping him to reach a capacity for making reparation, because this is something he is going to need to find—and it has got to do with the depressions, of course, because the suicidal bit has partly got to do with the impossibility of making reparation (there are all sorts of other side issues as well). He must feel that what he has done is irretrievable… in fantasy he must have committed many murders, so anything one can do that makes it possible for him to feel that reparation can be reached would help him more than any one other single thing. This will help him to tolerate consciousness of the bit of himself that may remain dangerous to himself and others.

Our aim is to have need assessment files, which will include the whole of the current population of a unit. These will be followed by later assessments, whenever these seem appropriate. We shall then be in a position to consider grouping in terms of emotional compatibility, and to avoid—what happens only too often—the disruption of an integrated group through the presence of a couple of 'frozen' ones, who are not only unable to get help themselves in this setting, but who will make it impossible for others to be helped.

I am well aware that there is a time factor involved, and that, as a consultant, my discussion groups with staff are built into the framework of the organization. Nevertheless, I cannot feel that these are the only circumstances in which need assessments can be made; and indeed, groups working under the leadership of the head of the house have been able to produce excellent assessments. All the same, I incline to the view that every residential unit should have consultancy available to help and support staff in their difficult task. I would suppose that one of these days there will be a training for consultancy in residential work, for which many social workers would be suitable candidates—but that is another story!

It would seem that in undertaking the task of assessment, no one person should be asked to do this alone; and that assessors, avoiding omnipotence in themselves, should not drift into collusion with the omnipotence of others as a means of escape from an intolerable load of responsibility.

10

Consultancy, 1971

This paper was written for an international seminar on consultancy in social work, held at York University in the summer of 1971.

Many years ago something happened to me which I have not forgotten. We were trying at that time to help a small delinquent character in the Mulberry Bush, who was known as Goblin. He had red hair, a bright pink face and a squint. He was goblin-shaped and very slightly spastic. I was talking about him with the psychiatrist who was supervising his treatment with us, Dr Barbara Woodhead, who is a psychoanalyst, one of the consultants who have done most to help the Bush, and to whom I personally am much indebted. Describing Goblin's behaviour, I spoke of his special song, 'Boiled beef and carrots'. He would ask in any situation, 'Would you like a song?', and there would inevitably follow 'Boiled beef and carrots'. Dr Woodhead laughed a little when I told her this, and remarked, 'He's really singing about himself, isn't he?—he *is* boiled beef and carrots, with that carroty hair and his red face!' For a moment I was stunned by a complicated feeling inside me, which I presently recognized as a mixture of envy and anger: envy that Dr Woodhead had understood something which I had missed—anger that I had failed to realize something so evident—evident as soon as she had pointed it out to me!

Recently something else happened to me which I found myself linking with this experience. I was talking with a small girl in a therapeutic school: we had been playing 'squiggles' (Winnicott's technique), and arising from her third squiggle she reached, and communicated, a terrible realization concerned with the beginning of her life (what Sechehaye would term 'symbolic realization'). Julia spoke loudly as her deep feelings burst their bonds and emerged in symbolic description. Now and then she paused for my response: since the meaning of the material was crystal clear, I could make statements based on the child's communications which were valid to her. During this dialogue there must have been a knock on my door which Julia and I were too absorbed to register: when presently she rose to go, we found a student waiting on the landing outside my room. Julia went her way, deep inside herself, and I apologized to the student–I had kept her waiting for several minutes. She came in, sat down, and there was silence for an instant. Then she said abruptly 'I have been eavesdropping... I heard what Julia and you were saying to each other. I want you to know now that I have *never* believed what you have written and said–I have never believed a word! Now, because I listened (I *did* knock, but you didn't hear) I know that children *can* talk like this ... that these things really happen.' She was very upset, but at the same time she experienced relief: she was actually communicating her envy of me–just the same kind of envy which I had experienced towards Dr Woodhead (and towards many other people who have known and understood more than I could myself).

These two episodes seem to me to typify the core of the consultant's problem–how to help and teach clients, without arousing conscious or unconscious envy, so intolerable that clients may be unable to make use of the help or the teaching, however valid and valuable this may be.

There has been much written about consultancy, although not enough concerning consultancy in residential work. Kaplan, Bettelheim and others have made important contributions on this subject: my own task in this paper is–as I have stated in my title–to describe my personal experience as a consultant, and also as one who has made use of available consultancy, especially in the residential treatment of severely deprived and unintegrated children and adolescents. It may well be that other workers will have had very different experiences, which they will realize and communicate in their own personal mode. This need not invalidate their work or my own. It is important to establish at once that I am writing (and usually do write) from a subjective standpoint–personal and special, rather than impersonal and general–although possibly we may be able to reach some general conclusions, such as my threshold statement that *envy is a factor which cannot be ignored in consultancy*. My aim is to share my own experiences with you, in the hope that by considering these, and conceptualizations based on actual work, we may be able to pinpoint the difficulties of consultancy in residential work and make some suggestions with regard to a hypothetical training in residential consultancy.

I have found through work over many years in residential places that in common with others I can be of far more use to children if I work through the staff, rather than attempt direct treatment by psychotherapy myself. This way of working does not preclude occasional 'key' sessions with children, either at their request or that of the worker involved (under no circumstances would I work with a child against his will). Now and then the child may need a brief series of such key sessions, usually at some crisis in evolvement. In the main, however, my discussions with staff members seem more appropriate to a situation in which the workers are in reality the therapists. My own role thus becomes supportive to the conscious involvements which are an essential part in the providing of primary experience. There is a grave danger that people working in a place can attribute to a consultant magical and omniscient powers, so that, relieved of responsibility, they can refer a child to the consultant, feeling thereafter that treatment is now 'out of their hands': at the same time, should the child act out or develop symptoms, they are likely to attribute such manifestations to the work of the psychotherapist. From the start, in working with a staff group I have found it essential to establish my own role as being supportive to the therapists in the place in *their* work with children. This role can be frustrating, and I have always had private patients of my own elsewhere, in order to enable me to tolerate working 'once removed' from children in residential places. The children themselves seem to reach a clear understanding about my contribution to the work of the place—even asking for certain problems to be discussed with me.

I was recently asked for a brief internal report on my task as a consultant at the Cotswold Community. In quoting from this, I hope to give some idea of the type of work needed in this field of residential work. The Cotswold Community used to be a rigid approved school, which over the past four years has been changed into a therapeutic community, under the directorship of Richard Balbernie.

MY TASK AS CONSULTANT AT THE COTSWOLD COMMUNITY

Initially, we saw my tasks to be (firstly) the provision of ego support in order to facilitate ego functioning in integrated children; (secondly) the containment of unintegrated children with provision of primary experience with which to build the self and achieve integration. These two tasks were to be carried out through work with both staff and boys. It was assumed that unintegrated children would form a small minority group in the place: this group would need, as soon as possible, to be insulated in order to receive appropriate treatment. The mixture of integrated and unintegrated boys was recognized as undesirable.

In the event, I was assigned to a house (St David's) consisting of very deprived and disturbed boys: this group was not yet separated in any way from the rest of the Community, but was self-selective in terms of gross disturbance as a common factor. I talked with the boys and with the staff invidually, until the staff themselves asked for group meetings with me. These staff groups became the nucleus of my work in the Community. My sessions with boys could—with their permission—be used to help staff to gain insight and to understand the need for teamwork in order to provide experience. These individual sessions were—and remain —of necessity brief (twenty to thirty minutes). I have found that where residential workers are themselves carrying out a therapeutic programme, sessions with individual boys have what I call a 'key' function, helping to open and deepen channels of communication between boys and workers.

St David s became presently the unit for unintegrated boys known as 'the Cottage'. Once this kind of insulation had been established, my task became more precise. By discussing weekly 'happenings' chosen by the Cottage team, I was able to help them to provide primary experience through individual adaptation to need, based on an early kind of dependence and involving localized regression within a relationship in a firmly structured containing environment. In this way, the team came to realize how disciplined any real therapeutic work must be, and the danger of collusion and the need for confrontation of a non-punitive kind. The team did good work, although naturally making many mistakes which with adequate support they could face. The development of an ego culture in the Cottage minimized authoritarian attitudes at one extreme, and subcultures at the other. The establishment of open communication between staff and boys reduced acting out; and the insulation and containment of this group of unintegrated boys enabled ego growth and strengthening in other groups within the Community.

For various reasons it was decided after a time that I should work in a similar consultant-tutor role in the remaining three house teams. My weekly discussion groups evolved into seminars, with learning based on the group experiences during the current week. Each group seminar lasts for forty-five minutes, with periods of from twenty to thirty minutes available (as before) for key sessions with boys (usually at their own request) and tutorials with team members – often the heads of houses. There is also a new housemothers' group. I have a close liaison with Trevor Blewett, the head of group living, who plans my day's work each week, and with whom I discuss my work in detail each Wednesday evening on the telephone, after my return home. I also have meetings with Mike Jinks, head of education. I meet Richard Balbernie, the Principal, frequently, and discuss problems and recommendations with him, both at the Cotswold and by telephone.

The development of a system of need assessment has enabled me to chart all houses on a basis of integrated or unintegrated: and if unintegrated, to chart the specific syndrome of deprivation (see chapters 8 and 9). From this 'inside diagnosis' we are now in a position to plan treatment on a basis of need, and to select with some certainty those boys to whom we can offer help. The work on need assessment is also enabling the staff to conceptualize and communicate what they are doing; and recently teams have begun to carry out these assessments themselves, checking results with me, so that we can plan treatment programmes in an exact way.

We hope to establish a plan for intake, which will exclude the occasional case which we cannot contain (a boy with a considerable psychotic pocket). Interviewing boys whose suitability is in doubt also comes into my task area.

This way of working brings me into contact with most people working in the Community, and enables me consequently to consider the total state of the place at any time. I am also in a position from which it is feasible to support the primary tasks in any group situation: at the same time recognizing and stopping what I have come to think of as the 'anti-tasks' which exist in every residential place, and which involve a collusive undertow of subculture (including adults and boys), undermining the ego functioning of the group and wrecking the primary task. The fact that there is a large proportion of unintegrated boys in the total group, a much larger proportion than we imagined originally, makes the presence of anti-task a constant hazard. I think that the fact I really respect the house teams, expecting them to carry out therapy themselves, helps them to accept my contribution to their increasingly skilled work.

TASK AND ANTI-TASK

The treatment of severely emotionally deprived children must take place in the context of what is happening in this place at this moment with this person (because unintegrated children have no realization of past or future). It is useless to confront a delinquent, for example, in retrospect; one must be *there* in the situation, anticipating acting out by the provision of communication. The consultant is of no use next day or next week – not even a few hours later – what is necessary is that the people in the place should have (or gain) the necessary skills and insight to carry out the work themselves.

The climate of a therapeutic school must always produce at least elements of a crisis culture – emotionally deprived children tend to live from crisis to crisis. The survival of such a place is often in question for obvious reasons. This leads to a paranoid position in which the grown-ups in the place – the treatment team – present a united front which is dependent on hostile outsiders to maintain the unity. The fact that there are really enemies, and others who say 'We are on your side', tends to perpetuate this unhappy state of affairs. A crisis culture of this sort is likely to breed anti-task, springing from those elements in children, staff and management which are unconsciously ranged against primary task.

I think there must always be anti-task present to some degree: the safety and survival of primary task is dependent upon enough ability and security to confront anti-task. If anti-task is not confronted, collusive anxiety can lead to states of panic, immobilization, and breakdown.

It is from anti-task activity that subculture grows, and there must always be some risks of this destructive phenomenon coming into being. The more secure the team groups, the smaller the risk, because confrontation of anti-task and subculture becomes felt as less dangerous. I think that collusive anxiety and collusion itself are great hazards in all residential work–including consultancy.

In a residential place, one often finds what I think of as a 'fallacy of a delusional equilibrium', maintained through collusive anxiety, so that anti-task may be covered, as it were, by a thin sheet of ice on which the people of the place skate at hazard.

The surfacing of anti-task is always painful, but the maintenance of a delusional equilibrium is self-destructive. It is better to have our feet on solid ground–however rocky–than to fear ice cracking beneath us. I find that supporting a team in the surfacing and confronting of anti-task can be a service which can strengthen the group ego.

In my report on my task in the Cotswold Community, I referred to 'need assessments'. The use of this kind of technique seems to me to be essential in focusing, as it does, the attention of the whole group (including the consultant) on the primary task–in our case, the provision of primary experience. On the basis that anti-task, acting out, and subcultures of all kinds tend to spring from a breakdown in real communication, it would seem of the utmost importance to keep all lines of communication open– between members of the team, between grown-ups and children, and between the consultant and all others in the place. The making of a need assessment involves the whole staff group of a residential unit, working with the consultant, and pooling resources in order to evaluate need.

Often insights are reached in the making of these assessments which are not only of value to the child under consideration, but also the treatment team themselves, throwing light on problems of delusional counter-transference–splitting mechanisms, for example–but in a way which is tolerable because it is indirect and shared. Such an approach seems to me to give child care workers a proper professional position in the scheme of things–the consultant being entirely dependent on the material brought forward by the unit team (see chapters 8 & 9).

In the need assessment questions I have used the terms to which

I am accustomed, giving explanations. In this way the workers involved have become used to distinctions such as 'empathy' compared with 'projective identification', 'personal guilt' (concern) as compared with 'fear of revenge' (talion guilt), and so on. At first, the going is slow and the reporting scant. Very soon, however, the task draws out the group potential. There is plenty of opportunity for argument and doubt. I find myself more easily accepted than in other forms of group reporting. As a result of discussing concepts such as 'merger', 'psychotic pocket' or 'burnt-out autism', workers wish to read papers and to reach further conceptualization, *because* this reaching out for more is based on their own experiences and realizations (I only provide ways of communicating these). The problem of envy of the consultant is much less likely to turn up, because anything that I can offer is at their disposal: I am not in a defended position. The need assessment which follows is on a small boy (aged seven) who has recently come to the Bush: this is a first assessment.

CHRISTOPHER'S NEED ASSESSMENT

I.Q. 100
Disruption. Yes.
Panic. One would certainly get the impression that there is some evidence of panic, but less frequent than when he arrived. He can spiral from an ordinary situation into panic—an area of panic in the total situation. The panic states he gets into are concerned with dependence. He may have used threats of panic state to get what he wants from grown-ups and then simulated panic states: his parents' reaction to this is to act out, and his mother will dissociate herself completely (we saw this happen here when the parents visited).
Classification: Unintegrated.
Guilt, personal concern: There is denial plus apparent outrage at being suspected (this is probably a very intellectual defence).
Dependence, trust: He is looking for the possibility of dependence and wanting to reach it: he is already dependent on Douglas Hawkins (child care worker) and this had grown, due to the hospital situation (i.e. when Christopher broke his leg and was in hospital overnight and most of the second day). When John Armstrong (headmaster) was carrying Christopher he was trusting

and really clinging.

Merger: No evidence.

Empathy: None.

Stress: There is verbal and physical aggression. He has a highly developed technique of logical argument; he keeps things under control by this kind of argument. He communicates in a stressful situation (the logical argument is probably a defence).

Communication: Symbolic communication at a fairly deep level—one example was concerned with the period when he was in hospital and away from the school for about twenty-six hours. He communicates more easily in moments of stress. There is non-verbal communication in which he indicates his need quite clearly. There is a little bond which continues with B. D-D.—he appeared at the door of her room at a time when she had someone else there and was not able to give time to Christopher, she explained. He went off, then returned and asked for some paper and a pencil. Since then, from time to time, he comes and is supplied with sheets of paper and a pencil—as yet this situation has not advanced in any way.

Identification: Quite a lot of projective identification—Christopher asked for his clean clothes with the firm intention of getting ready for the arrival of another boy's parents and going out with them (this, of course, was not allowed). He aims at obtaining experience secondhand. He tends to identify with his father: and Christopher does 'switch off', and this could be identification with his mother, who dissociates.

Depression: There is not a depressed mood.

Aggression: Yes, verbal and physical.

Capacity for play: On the whole, his play is narcissistic: he enjoys play with water, paint, sand (he bends the rules, cheats).

Capacity for learning: He presumably does learn from experience—he has got as far as he has by insisting on being taken care of; he has fought for this care by rumpus-raising and any other means that work, and for a while, as long as these methods work for him, he will continue to use them. There are signs that this particular mechanism is declining as he finds his needs are being met (at a mealtime, on being given his milk, he will say 'And fill it right to the top'). There was a little game with B.D-D., when Christopher was in bed, with circus, clowns, masks: B.D-D.

suggested that it might not now be so necessary for Christopher to hide behind a mask–he smiled.

Self preservation: He does get hurt a lot: he cuts himself, falls over (the broken leg now, and various other accidents).

False self. (Comment from B.D.-D.)–A false-self child who will get to regression and deep dependence–probably rather total regression. From the description of him in bed and what I met of him in bed, I would think that the accidents, disasters, illnesses and anything else he can collect of this sort are, in fact, opportunities for regression and that he can then be at peace. One gets the impression that he makes good use of all these things that are happening to him.

One must look for adaptations leading to regression; notice anything he says or indicates about things that are suitable for him –like the cup of milk that has to be filled right up–this is obviously something important to him. Slowly, one hopes, he will establish stepping stones to get his regression, and accidents and goodness knows what, and that seems unnecessary.

He will have to reach considerable ego strength to be able to cope with his parents–even assuming they do remain together.

Such a child can arouse much hostility in a treatment unit because of his initial *un*dependence; his apparent ability to do without us is a threat to people who want to be of use to deprived children.

The team at the Bush have considerable insight, and can comment on their own defences, and to some extent clear them out of the way. The shared experience of the need assessment helps the team and myself to orientate more directly and simply to the now defined task, to provide a regression for Christopher, with stepping stones of adaptation: for example, the paper and pencil, the full cup of milk, and the symbolic communication. The special kind of reliability which he is meeting from everyone (especially from Douglas) will lead him to put down further stepping stones towards regression. The regression itself may well be managed by several people who will support each other in order to ensure continuity of care and symbolic provision. My main task will be to support the team and to share realizations with them as we go along together. This kind of support really has much in common with that needed by 'the ordinary devoted mother', the difference being that this is conscious and professional work, where intuition is not enough.

CONCLUSION

As a consultant in residential work, I find that my own considerable experience of working as an 'insider'—a therapist *in* a therapeutic community—is invaluable, now that I work as an outsider coming into the place. My analysis, and the tremendous help I have received myself from consultants, help me to empathize with others in consultancy with me. Finally, my conviction that therapy in a residential place must be carried out by the people in the place helps to avoid a 'we' and 'they' situation, in which massive defences and counter-defences can cripple open communication between consultant and treatment team.

I I

The management of violence
in disturbed children, 1971

This paper was read late in 1970 as my contribution to a seminar on violence run by the Department of Health and Social Security. The material at the end of the paper was an experiment for use in discussion groups, and was sufficiently successful for me to wish to repeat the technique.

An outbreak of violence in any human being, grown-up or child, is always frightening to a degree, because we know, consciously or intuitively, that here is the expression of feelings so terrible as not to be containable. We are sometimes conscious of violence in ourselves which we cannot always successfully contain, but which most of the time is deep in our unconscious: potential, but untapped. The explosion of another's violence reminds us of this potential in ourselves, perhaps of occasions when even to some much lesser extent our own violence has come into our consciousness and may have to some degree been acted out in our environment.

During the first year of life, babies change from being contained (by their mothers and the holding environment) to becoming 'containers'. There are no feelings stronger, deeper, or more overwhelming than those which are already experienced at this early date. The 'ordinary devoted mother' (Winnicott) can contain the baby's rage and her own feelings as long as this is necessary – until the baby can contain his own feelings. Many of the children in our care have not become containers: at five, ten or fifteen years they may still need a lot of containment in order to integrate into whole, containing people. In the meantime, they are liable to act out their intolerably violent emotions in many ways, damaging to other people, themselves and their environment.

Winnicott defined panic as 'unthinkable anxiety'. Much violence is caused by panic states: *thinking* is an essential way of containing feelings. Communication of such thoughts to others can be an unknown safety valve – if the thoughts are not there, they cannot

123

be communicated; the anxiety is then so terrible and primitive as to be unthinkable, and the child reaches a panic state in which he may be totally immobilized, or dreadfully active.

One could say that the communication of violent feelings in words to another person is a symbolic way of finding a person able and willing to contain the child and his feelings.

A neurotic, integrated child (i.e. a well-established 'container', with boundaries to himself and an inner reality within him) will be able to make such communication if it can reach consciousness. An integrated child has many means at his disposal of containing terrible feelings. For example, he can repress his violent aggression, or he can convert this into a symptom, or he can sublimate the aggression, putting it to some useful purpose. Usually a neurotic, integrated child will only experience the occasional twinge of panic with which we are all familiar; he is only likely to explode briefly and in a localized way into violence, and is usually able to put his feelings into words—even though these may be screamed.

The deprived, unintegrated child has no such resources. Where the integrated can *respond* to crisis, the unintegrated *reacts* to what he feels to be the threat of total annihilation. For him, conflict is not the question, but rather survival, not only of himself but of *everything*. Annihilation of the kind I am describing is something comparable to 'the end of the world'. Even integrated people can experience this dread now and then, but they are not constantly exposed to the threat of infinite destruction, in the way that deprived and unintegrated children seem to be; nor do they have to manage annihilating forces within themselves. Unintegrated people simply *overflow* into violence: integrated people disintegrate into areas of violence—they are much less at risk than the former group.

At the present time, groups in residential places are a mixture of integrated and unintegrated—this demands tolerance of a high degree of incompatibility by children and staff: I have written elsewhere about this (see chapter 3), and would draw your attention to this aspect of the film *John*[1], in which an integrated toddler was exposed to the full blast of unintegrated peers, with appalling

[1] See note to page 72.

results. There would perhaps be less disastrous effects of separation if the dangers of incompatible mixing were more generally recognized.

In any community home there are likely to be several unintegrated, uncontaining children who are certain to break down into violence which will harm others and themselves. Unintegrated children are not especially disturbed by these explosions which come into their 'scene'. Integrated children are terribly threatened by violence because they *can disintegrate*, which unintegrated ones cannot do because they have never been 'in one piece' and are not whole people.

The grown-ups involved in such a situation are also frightened and disturbed, and this can affect them in all sorts of ways, depending on individual personalities. Institutionalization and hierarchical management are defences against these fears. Workers may 'switch off' feelings, depersonalize, become cold and pseudo-objective, and hand over the 'happening' to superiors, or become violent themselves.

Descriptions of violent behaviour in children tend to be detached, in a way which leaves the grown-up in a superior position. The grown-up may become 'angry' and the child has a 'temper tantrum'. The grown-up asserts, in such a context, that the violence is that of childhood–there is a deep unwillingness to face the fact that grown-ups are not so different in reality, and are also capable of having temper tantrums . It is difficult for a grown-up to admit that he has behaved violently towards a child, because he feels himself to be too mature for such behaviour. Really it becomes essential for the person working with children to be well aware of the possible violence within himself. We all know the gentle, patient person who arranges (unconsciously, of course) for children to act out his violence while he stays calm and 'good'.

'Punishment' is often a rationalization of violence–grown-ups can act out, denying the real causes within themselves which lead to their violent actions.

If one can see all acting out as a breakdown in communication –an area in which the individual cannot contain and think about his feelings, then one's attitude is more honest and less defended, so that one is actually more free to take appropriate action and to make comments which are valuable to the child.

Thinking about children and violence, I find myself considering two phases: (1) before the violent act takes place, and (2) after the act of violence has been committed. Anticipation of violence calls for good observation, empathy, and a feeling for dynamics – 'one thing leads to another'. Too often 'another' has been reached without 'one thing' having been observed and registered.

Panic states are, in a sense, psychosomatic. One can observe physical symptoms in a child one has come to know. Pallor, trembling, change of voice and breathing, dilation of the eyes, and a desperate restlessness may all be signals of an approaching storm. At this stage, insulation and containment may save the child and the environment from disaster. There was much to criticize in the film '*Warrendale*'[1], but here at least an effort was made to contain the child and his feelings *in time*. The point is often made that 'nothing has happened to cause the outbursts of violence'. The truth is that we may not have realized what has happened to the child in terms of his inner reality. *Something*–a look, a word, a circumstance, may have set up a chain of associations which will have forced him to remember through feeling 'other voices, other rooms' (Capote).

Emotionally deprived children are traumatized at a stage so early that they cannot realize, symbolize or conceptualize what has happened to them: they 'remember' only through feeling. *There is no way of containing traumata*. This is how I understand the aetiology of panic states and the violence which springs from them.

Panic is contagious: adults, even experienced workers, can catch panic from children. This contagious quality is generally recognized in crowd panics (football disasters, fires in cinemas or theatres, for example) but is less easily seen in individual panic states. This infection partly explains the immobilization which can beset grown-ups confronted by violence. One has to hold on to one's identity, to guard the frontiers of one's self in a situation. To *contain* the child and his violence is not the same as to merge with him.

There is a tendency to identify with violence in a very primitive and unconscious way. I knew a family once–all grown up–which contained a schizophrenic brother, hospitalized from time to

---

[1] '*Warrendale*', Allan King, 1967.

time, but for the most part living at home and causing chaos. An elder brother who owned a shop had just installed a large plate-glass show window; the schizophrenic one, in a moment of rage, smashed the new plateglass window to smithereens. When the family told me of this disaster, there was unmistakeable envy in their voices—envy of the ill brother who could do this terrible, violent act and 'get away with it'!

Often, in the therapeutic institutions where I work, children have said to me 'I really don't know how I came to do it' in describing some act of violence. But often, going carefully over the events of that day, we have been able to find a terrible build-up of unnoticed tension, leading to final breakdown. The child may even have been actually conscious of the tension and its causes, but there has been no opportunity to communicate this to a grown up in time. So here the child and I are, in retrospect, trying to talk about what should have been in the future and is now in the past.

A boy, Tom, aged nine, at the Mulberry Bush some years ago broke windows for no apparent cause, and with tremendous violence. It was finally possible to link these explosions with a breakdown in communication with his mother. When this happened—when no letter arrived—Tom became convinced that she was dead. Waiting for the news of her death produced tension and panic so terrific that the smashing of glass produced temporary relief.

I have spoken of moments of panic violence in integrated children, and of prolonged panic states leading to violence in unintegrated ones: there is another more rare category of violence, but one which I suspect is more common than one would suppose. This is the violence displayed by a more or less integrated child who has a psychotic pocket. This pocket of madness is not emotionally linked to the rest of him: he has integrated 'round a hole'. This means in effect that he can suddenly depart, as it were, into the mad bit of himself, so that an apparently well-behaved, sensible boy can suddenly commit violent crimes; and having done so, return into the major, sane part of himself. The mad bit is hidden from himself, as it is from others, although there are unmistakeable clues as to the presence of the psychotic pocket.

We are concerned here today with all these kinds of violence;

whatever form they may take, as we meet children's outbursts in residential treatment. All violence has a quality of orgasm: it is preceded by an intense spiral of excitement, leading to climax and followed by relief and subsidence. Panic is, at its climax, a kind of traumatic orgasm. Violent behaviour has always sexual undertones, sometimes conscious ones. The sexuality can, however, range from displaced infantile greed (delinquency) to genital sexuality (rape). There are often particular fantasies which accompany the violent behaviour. Essentially, however, I believe that children are swept along by violence: they can do terrible things in cold blood, but these are usually sadistic and not necessarily *violent*. Violence, as I understand the phenomenon, implies a loss of control, a helpless rage.

The management of violence, as I have indicated earlier in this paper, has two phases. Ideally, there should be anticipation, so that the violent act does not have to take place. Failing anticipation, there must be containment and control of the violent out-of-control child in a panic. Essential at both stages is communication: although the child does not seem to hear a word one is saying at the time, he will remind one, years later, of communications made in such circumstances. All acting out is broken down communication, and we can build a bridge even in a welter of flailing legs and arms, gnashing teeth, spitting mouth, and snarling, shrieking voice. *If you can communicate, he can hear.* What one communicates depends on each individual child and the context, but there are basic assumptions which we can start from—the child's helplessness, the echo of early trauma, the helpless infantile rage (however big he may be). So that, for example, when a boy yells 'Leave me alone' it is appropriate to reply 'I promise not to leave you.' The most valuable thing we can do in such circumstances is to continue to be alive, reliable and concerned. I always hold on when a child is in a panic state: I hold his hand, trying not to lose my hold, and I continue to communicate. I may have an arm round the child. We may be standing or sitting; he may be lying on his back, or whirling around me; but I try to hold on, and if I do lose my hold on his hand I re-establish this as soon as I can. This is not so difficult, because part of him *wants* to be held. Presently, he will be the one who is doing the holding, and the worst is then over.

Anticipation very often *precipitates* the panic state: but we are then in a position of strength to hold the child and his rage, and to prevent the violent act which would have followed. Really, every act of violence which we have to consider in retrospect is basically a failure in management.

Bruno Bettelheim, in his book *The Children of the Dream* concerning Kibbutzim, which some of you may have read, writes:

> Conversely, being sure of one's place might explain another striking contrast to what is typical in our society, and why kibbutz childhood is such a happy age. Not once did I observe any physical fighting among kibbutz children. Not once – beyond the age when they push each other down in the playpen – did I see a child pushing another, not to mention hitting with hand or object. This does not occur in the kibbutz. I asked about it repeatedly, and the answer was always the same; while there are disagreements, they never go beyond verbal expression. There are no fights about things like who comes first, or who sits where. Compared with the frequent fighting that seems typical in our society among pre-school and grammar-school children, life in the kibbutz at this age is peaceful indeed.
>
> Of course, it helps that there are no possessions to fight over and no social distinctions. But much of the fighting at this age in our society originates in the child's feeling that he has no place that is rightfully his. He must fight first to assert it and then to maintain it – whether the unending fight explodes in physical violence, or is carried on in more hidden form.

Here we might pause to consider Robert Ardry's 'Territorial Imperative', which in human beings means basically 'room' – emotional and physical – in which to be an individual. Very often this is *not* available to severely deprived children. On the other hand, the idealized institutionalization which dominates a kibbutz denies the child the right to be an individual.

In this connection it seems important to consider what Winnicott wrote about depression.

> The main thing is that depression indicates that the individual is accepting responsibility for the aggressive and destructive elements in human nature. This means that the depressed person has a capacity for holding a certain amount of guilt (about matters that are chiefly unconscious), and this allows of a sear-

ching round for an opportunity for constructive activity.

Our violent deprived children have not reached this position. I have spoken of containers; destructive feelings and guilt must be contained if the person is to have a real identity.

I want now to consider the actual presence of violence and how we can manage the child and his violence in a therapeutic and non-punitive or retaliatory way. I assume this is the problem for all of us: we may understand the causes of violence, but how do we actually deal with violent behaviour?

Some years ago James, a ten-year-old, was provoked by a younger boy, on whom he then made what was really a murderous attack; if he could have killed the younger boy he would have done so. Intervention took place instantly, but we had not been quick enough to anticipate disaster. I spent the next hour trying to keep in touch, physically and emotionally, with James, who was tied up in knots on his bed, shrieking obscenities (the violence had taken place in a dormitory). I kept on talking: about James, his pain and anguish, his intolerable panic state. He did not seem to register what I was saying until suddenly he screamed at me, 'People like you don't understand people like me—I've murdered love!' He felt that he had destroyed everything.

Another boy aged thirteen, who was very tall and strong, took up a large lump of coal and threw it at my head—he was only a few yards away. I could see that he was going to do this, but there was no one near enough to intervene: so I froze in my tracks and the coal whistled past my ear. A moment later he was stumbling over to me, white and crying. He said, 'I've always known I'd have to try and kill you.' His mother had left him and his father.

There was a ten-year-old, Jeremy, who was epileptic and very disturbed. When he first came to us from a mental hospital, he would stand in the middle of his bed, swinging a full hotwater bottle round his head, and shrieking, 'I'm going to throw it at you'. I used to stand at the end of the bed, talking to him, and ultimately he would burst into tears, throwing the hot bottle on to the floor. His parents had been terrified of him. In this case holding was not necessary.

Peter used to hit people—children and grown-ups—with all his strength: this was so sudden as to be impossible to anticipate.

He was a large tough thirteen-year-old. We discovered that he could not believe that he could *reach* anyone: the blow was a distorted communication. Interpretation brought him enough trust to reach out to others.

Compare these outbursts of violence with the case of a small patient of mine, Edward, aged four, who described the monsters in the garden who threatened him at night. These were his own uncontainable violent feelings, projected on to his environment. It is true that Edward did not commit violent acts, but neither (at that time) could he contain these terrible feelings. He became threatened by them from outside himself; he took up a paranoid position, living in anguish and fear.

All these children were unintegrated: the violence of integrated people is much more localized—in fact they partially *disintegrate* into violence. The more integrated the person, the quicker and easier will it be to re-establish thinking and communication, thereby enabling the child to *complete the experience*. I think that the concept of the complete experience is important in this connection. Nightmares are usually interrupted dreams—the dreamer can find no solution, so he wakes. In the same way the child can feel unable to resolve some intolerable situation: he tries to 'wake up', to escape from the terrible stress, but he *is* awake, so he collapses into panic. As I have said earlier, this can take the form of violence or immobilization, even the loss of consciousness.

In all these examples I have given there has been a breakdown in communication: the restoration of thinking in words restores stability, and makes the dangerous feelings containable. It is an awful fact that well-meaning people can provoke violence by irrelevant and inappropriate value judgments. For example, a child desperately trying to reach communication with a grown-up may be termed 'attention seeking'. When *we* ask someone 'Are you paying attention?' we mean 'Are you listening?' Of course children need, and ask for, our attention: what they are saying is urgent. Equally, when an infuriated youngster shouts an answer to some accusation or criticism, he may well be told not to 'answer back'. I have never been able to understand this ridiculous phrase. This kind of grown-up behaviour can trigger off violence in every form: people are shutting off the safety-valve of speech. Perhaps one of the problems lies in the fact that one tends to understand

what a child is saying (or what he is likely to say) in such circumstances to be an accusation. If, instead of accusing us, he attacks
someone else, or smashes the place to smithereens, or sets fire
to a barn, *we do not have to understand* what he might have said.
We can just be angry with him for what he has done, and get rid
of our own feelings of guilt.

Actually, the establishment of communication with disturbed
children always leads to a torrent of accusation in the first place,
directed against ourselves and everyone else. It is essential in
therapeutic work to be able to accept the reality of the *feelings*
expressed, and not to waste time arguing about the facts, which
are probably quite otherwise but are in any case irrelevant.

How one responds to violence or to communication of violent
feelings depends on the kind of person one happens to be. One
person may say 'How can you talk about your mother like this?'
when in reality the grown-up would like to say some pretty awful
things about his own mother but is not in a position to do so.
Or he can say 'But you *know* Miss A is always so kind to you . . .'
when everyone knows that Miss A does not get on at all well
with this particular child.

A terrifying fact is that behaviour can be interpreted incorrectly
as violent, and such interpretation can be accepted by the child
on to whom it is projected. A boy in a residential place met a staff
wife out walking with her dog. She was carrying a chain lead.
She did not know Johnnie, who had just arrived, but greeted him.
He trailed along behind her, making vague remarks; he asked to
carry the chain, which she gave to him. He walked on, swinging
the chain, and presently he said that he wanted to show her a
damaged puppy nearby. She followed him, but there was no
puppy. She asked him for the chain, which he gave to her, and
then he took off his jersey, twisted it, and swung this instead of
the chain 'as though it were a rope'. There were various myths
concerned with violence and this boy, and when this episode was
reported to me there was the implication that violence was present
just below the surface. In fact, the 'damaged puppy' represented
Johnnie himself; the chain or lead and the 'rope' of jersey were
links to a grown-up, a seeking for dependence, in a strange place
(I knew enough about Johnnie to be sure of this). If Johnnie had
collected this projection (he did not) he could have *felt* that he

was a violent person.

On rare occasions a woman may be really threatened by a violent boy in a residential place. He may need to be physically controlled for her safety and his own. Whenever possible she should call for help from a man, rather than involve herself in physical struggle with the child. Nothing is more disastrous than for a woman to lose her role and act like a man, using her strength to overcome a boy. Some women seem to need to show how physically strong they are, but in doing so they lose their emotional strength (in the same way it is sad when a mother has to be a father to her son).

Men may use much more strength than is necessary in order to control a violent child: perhaps because they assert their masculine power which is threatened; perhaps because there are homosexual elements present, although unconscious. In the same way, women can be sexually aroused by a struggle with a violent boy or girl. Because this is unconscious they may provoke this sort of battle in order to obtain sexual excitement. Really it is very seldom necessary to use physical force, although holding a child firmly with one's arm round him, or holding his hand, may be very necessary. To react to violence with violence is only likely to promote more violence: there is a narrow margin between 'strength' and 'violence'.

There is also what I think of as 'institutionalized violence', the extreme versions of which are execution and killing in battle. Here, violent acts are rationalized by organization and hierarchy. One sees this in the use of violence in punishment. Such acts– beating, for example–are organized with great care, with respect for hierarchy, rules and ceremonies: in this way the face of violence is masked. In Ireland in the eighteenth century the hangman wore a horrific animal mask in order to hide his identity from society.

I have been in institutions where there is excellent order and control, reasonably benign authority, and no sign of violence in management of children. On the other hand, the children seem too quiet, too passive: on further investigation I have found that in such a place the newcomer is exposed to violent treatment so that he becomes afraid. There is then no need for more than threat –discipline and control can be easily maintained. One is reminded of a disturbed small child who shows one a fly which he has already half stunned, saying, 'Look how tame it is–it doesn't want to leave me.' Of course there is a lot of collusion involved in such a state of affairs: people are often thankful to wear blinkers.

Gang violence in a place has much in common with this kind of institutionalized violence. Children in a delinquent group in a subculture will also commit violent acts (under cover of 'initiation', for example). The leader of such a gang is liable to have a psychotic pocket. Subcultures flourish in a punitive climate in which violence is implicit when not explicit. Some people assume that this kind of subculture is 'part of the scene'. This is not a valid assumption: lack of communication between staff and children can lead to the first signs of subculture. There is no reason why such a growth should flourish unless there is collusive anxiety present in the adult group (who will have a subculture of their own). Confrontation, recognition of the 'storm centre'–the delinquent hero–and establishment of real communication, will remove the need for the subculture; which, in a group, is rather like autism in an individual.

When a grown-up hits a child in a moment of rage, this is a violent act which must never be denied. Nobody ought to strike a child, but if this happens the fact should be communicated to others, and the child should understand clearly that the grown-up has been unable to control or contain his anger. Certainly a blow in anger is preferable to a planned beating, because we are not deceiving the child or ourselves in the former circumstances.

You will have noticed that I have drifted over a wide field in this chapter. The point is that this *is* a large field; violence is as it were the infra-red of every spectrum. The possibility of violence is always implicit in every situation that involves people in relation to one another, because violence is there in all of us. The more conscious we can be of our own potential violence, the less likely are we to become violent ourselves, and the more able shall we be to understand and manage violence in others when this is necessary.

AN EPISODE OF VIOLENCE

Henry, aged eight, was a very disturbed boy of high intelligence, placed in a residential special school for maladjusted children. This was the first day of the summer term. His mother had brought him on the afternoon before to the station to meet staff from the school, who had come to London to bring children back to the school in —— shire: Henry and his mother had arrived just in time to catch the train.

The night before, Henry had overheard a terrible outburst of anger between his parents, during which his father had threatened once again to leave him and his mother. His mother had spoken softly, and he could only hear the murmur of her voice going on and on.

After returning to the school, there had not been a suitable moment for Henry to speak about his anxiety to a 'special' grown-up because of the general rush of settling down in the school. The child care worker to whom he would have communicated his anxiety as he had done in the past was on leave. This worker was kind and gentle: she always listened intently, was appalled by his father's outbursts and deeply sorry for his mother–it comforted Henry to talk to her. When Henry's mother came to the school, Mary, this worker, would listen to her complaints about her husband with deep sympathy. Henry's father rarely visited the school: Mary did not talk with him in her soft, quiet voice–she could not bear to do so.

On the morning in question, Henry was no longer thinking about his worry, but was chatting to other children and to the child care staff, who were helping them to get dressed. One of the children said 'I wonder if it's going to rain ...' and Henry said 'Of course not, look how blue the sky is' (there were quite a few dark clouds). He was not hungry at breakfast. At assembly, the children said the Lord's Prayer: towards the end, Henry stopped saying the well-known words, and did not even think them inside himself. Later, his teacher, who was a man whom Henry knew and liked well, asked the children to write an essay about 'My Holidays'. Suddenly the whole horror of the situation at home came back into his mind: he sat, staring in front of him, and was startled when the teacher asked him 'What's wrong?' Henry started to write 'I went to the zoo ...' At lunch time, he still was not hungry. He felt awfully full, stuffed, it was as though something was choking him. People asked him if he was ill, but he shook his head. Anything said to him now seemed like a blow, which made him wince, and any contact became intolerable. He no longer knew what was causing him such anguish which seemed to engulf him. He went out after lunch into the playground in a daze.

Suddenly another boy punched him in the back. This was not a hard punch, but Henry felt a burning behind his nose; he shivered all over and turned white. In an instant, he had thrown himself screaming on the other boy, knocked him down, and tried to strangle him. Staff intervened, and with difficulty pulled Henry away from the boy he was attacking and held him while he screamed and kicked. They tried to understand what had gone wrong, but he was too distressed to speak or even think. He was put to bed for the rest of the day. On the following morning he got up as usual... .

Index